Marx

Towards the Centre
of Possibility

Marx
Towards the Centre of Possibility

Edited, translated, and with an introduction by Gavin Walker

Kōjin Karatani

London • New York

With support from the Japan Foundation
This English-language edition published by Verso 2020
Originally published in Japanese as *Marukusu sono kanōsei no chūshin*, 1974
© Kōjin Karatani 2020
Translation and Introduction © Gavin Walker 2020

All rights reserved

The moral rights of the author and translator have been asserted

1 3 5 7 9 10 8 6 4 2

Verso
UK: 6 Meard Street, London W1F 0EG
US: 20 Jay Street, Suite 1010, Brooklyn, NY 11201
versobooks.com

Verso is the imprint of New Left Books

ISBN-13: 978-1-78873-058-7
ISBN-13: 978-1-78873-779-1 (LIBRARY)
ISBN-13: 978-1-78873-059-4 (UK EBK)
ISBN-13: 978-1-78873-060-0 (US EBK)

British Library Cataloguing in Publication Data
A catalogue record for this book is available from the British Library

Library of Congress Cataloging-in-Publication Data
Names: Karatani, Kōjin, 1941- author.
Title: Marx : towards the centre of possibility / Kojin Karatani.
Other titles: Marukusu sono kanōsei no chūshin. English
Description: London ; Brooklyn, NY : Verso, 2020. | Includes bibliographical references and index. | Summary: "Originally published in 1974, Kojin Karatani's Marx: Towards the Centre of Possibility has been amongst his most enduring and pioneering works in critical theory. Written at a time when the political sequences of the New Left had collapsed into crisis and violence, with widespread political exhaustion for the competing sectarian visions of Marxism from 1968, Karatani's Marx laid the groundwork for a new reading, unfamiliar to the existing Marxist discourse in Japan at the time. Karatani's Marx takes on insights from semiotics, deconstruction, and the reading of Marx as a literary thinker, treating Capital as an intervention in philosophy that could be read as itself a theory of signs. Marx is unique in this sense, not only because of its importance in post-68 Japanese thought, but also because the heterodox reading of Marx that Karatani debuts in this text, centered on his theory of the value-form, will go on to form the basis of his globally-influential work"– Provided by publisher.
Identifiers: LCCN 2019044487 | ISBN 9781788730587 (paperback) | ISBN 9781788737791 (library binding) | ISBN 9781788730600 (ebook)
Subjects: LCSH: Socialism. | Marxian economics. | Communism and literature. | Marx, Karl, 1818-1883.
Classification: LCC HX73 .K36413 2020 | DDC 335.4–dc23
LC record available at https://lccn.loc.gov/2019044487

Typeset in Sabon by MJ & N Gavan, Truro, Cornwall
Printed and bound by CPI Group (UK) Ltd, Croydon CR0 4YY

Contents

Acknowledgements — vii
Note on the Translation — ix
'Karatani's Marx' by Gavin Walker — xi

Preface to the English Edition — xxix

Chapter One — 1

Chapter Two — 15

Chapter Three — 35

Chapter Four — 49

Chapter Five — 65

Chapter Six — 87

Chapter Seven — 103

Index — 113

Acknowledgements

I would like to thank above all Kōjin Karatani himself, for discussions and exchanges on the present book, and for agreeing to the translation of this early work of his, which has had such an important effect on the development of critical theory in Japan.

Thanks to Michael Bourdaghs and Ken Kawashima for their support of the project, to Sebastian Budgen, Rosie Warren, Cian McCourt, and others at Verso for their editorial support, and to Rachel and Anne for their love and support.

I initially translated the text while I was a faculty fellow at the Institute for the Public Life of Art & Ideas at McGill University, and finished the final editing of the text while a visiting researcher at the Institute for Research in the Humanities at Kyoto University, a wonderful place to work. I thank Kenta Ohji for his invitation, and all the staff of the Institute for their support during my stay.

The translation and publication were made possible in part by support from the Japan Foundation UK, who provided a Translation Grant, and by support from the Social Sciences and Humanities Research Council of Canada.

Note on the Translation

Throughout this volume, Japanese language is transliterated according to the modified Hepburn system. Karatani's original text, like the bulk of Marxist theoretical writing in Japanese until recently, has only a very limited reference apparatus, with no bibliography, and no specific citations. For this English-language edition, all citations in the text have been sourced to original texts, or to their major English-language translations.

All texts of Marx and Engels have been referred to the editions of record: the *Marx-Engels Collected Works* (Moscow, London, New York: Progress Publishers, Lawrence & Wishart, and International Publishers) in English, and the *Marx-Engels Werke* (Berlin: Dietz) and *Marx-Engels Gesamtausgabe* (Berlin: Dietz) in German. I have added occasional footnotes marked [Trans.] for terms and concepts that Karatani mentions but that are not developed in the text, particularly in relation to the Japanese-language theoretical situation.

In Japanese-language Marxist theoretical writing, Marx's economic abbreviations are typically retained in the style of the German original. Hence W is used for *Ware*, G for *Geld*, Pm for *Produktionsmittel*, A for *Arbeitskraft*, etc. I have changed these to the standard English usage: C = commodity, M = money, Mp = means of production, L = labour power, c = constant capital, v = variable capital, s = surplus value.

In general, I have endeavoured to avoid a mode of translation – which is, to be formally consistent with Karatani's argument in this text, nothing more than one particular reading protocol – that accentuates the linguistic distance of the text. By that I mean something quite simple. There is a mode of translation that seeks, at all times, to render opaque *yet distant* the original text in its translated form. Such a mode emphasizes 'untranslatable' terms, terms in the original left *transliterated*, forms of expression that seek to establish a stylistic difference that the reader is free (although also propelled) to regard as emblems of cultural divergence. I reject wholly this mode of translation, not because it is 'less accurate' – after all, 'accuracy' is nearly impossible to coherently assess in translation – but because it places the text within an economy of meaning that evades textuality in favour of a first-order explanatory mechanism of 'cultural difference'. Needless to say, this apparent 'cultural difference' is itself never explained, but simply relied upon as a given, initial stratum of meaning that is posited at the outset, or strictly speaking, pre-posited. Karatani's work is impossible to assess on such a basis. The context, properly speaking, of this work is the global spread of anti-humanist, anti-essentialist critical theory that entered the world conceptual scene in the late 1940s, and that has conditioned a crucial segment of intellectual history ever since. In that sense, I do not exoticize Karatani's writing, which is clear, straightforward, and although influenced by the current of deconstruction dominant at Yale in the 1970s when he was there, never attempted to appropriate the Derridean style. The book should be read absolutely without reliance on any conception of Japanese-ness as a supposed explanatory mechanism, but instead with an understanding that the Japanese tradition of social theory was itself undergoing remarkable *international* transformations at the time.

Karatani's Marx

Gavin Walker

Often, one translates a book because it is topical for our moment in an untimely fashion; what appeared at the forefront of the historical process in one part of the world may later come to dominate at another moment elsewhere. Other times, one translates a book because of its intellectual-historical value; texts frequently concretize and concentrate in their appearance a whole continent of thought surrounding their moment of emergence. At yet other points, one might translate a book whose mode of expression is unique, distinctive, or rare in our world. In all cases, the 'value' of the translation is linked to some aspect of the historicity of the text, be it of immediate, historical, or logical importance. Kōjin Karatani's *Marx* is all of these things at once: an exceptionally important work in intellectual-historical terms, a distinctive reading of Marx whose insights remain powerful, and an early key to the later developments of his thought, already amply represented in the English language.

Today, Karatani himself needs little introduction as a thinker. Since the 1970s, he has been at the forefront of Japanese intellectual life, producing numerous influential works of social theory, literary criticism, political thought, and intellectual history, among them the 1974 *Marukusu sono kanōsei no chūshin* (Marx: Towards the Centre of Possibility). This early book, which pioneered a new theoretical role for Marx in the Japanese situation, both drawing on and moving away from the heavily methodological analyses of the postwar

Japanese tradition of Marxist theory (represented by thinkers such as Uno Kōzō and Hiromatsu Wataru), paved the way for a new opening of critical theory, in the broad sense, in Japanese intellectual life. Karatani's influence on multiple generations of thinkers cannot be overstated, both for his own original 'reading protocols' and conceptual innovations, as well as his organizational and editorial role, founding and animating the widely influential journal *Hihyō kūkan* (Critical Space) throughout the 1990s. Edited in collaboration with the influential critic Akira Asada, *Hihyō kūkan* or *Critical Space* played an exceptional – and rare – role for the intellectual space of contemporary Japanese thought. Published for roughly fifteen years, from its founding in 1991 to its final issue in the mid 2000s, *Critical Space* distinguished itself above all for the remarkable curation of texts that Karatani and Asada undertook, its influential transcripts of group discussions and round-tables, in some cases field-defining, and the unique mixture of theoretical work that was possible in the journal, ranging from Marxian political economy to philosophy, social theory, literature, music, architecture, art and more. In a sense, since its dissolution, other journals which overlapped in content – such as *Gendai shisō: Revue de la pensée d'aujourd'hui* (published since the early 70s by Seidosha, and itself an important site for the development of critical theory in Japan) – have been in a process of retreat, and, I would say, especially in a process of de-internationalization. Karatani and Asada's unique mixture of great influence domestically along with their international links provided a complex and powerful *space* of critique that has yet to be replicated.

As Karatani has frequently pointed out – and as he does again in the new 2019 preface to this edition – his own texts on Marx have tended to appear at moments in which Marx was *least* on the theoretical agenda. In some sense, the publication of this work in 2020 is untimely in a classically doubled sense. On the one hand, it is a voice out of time, a voice from the 1970s, immersed in a theoretical situation that could not be further from that of the Anglophone world today. In another sense, it is untimely, because it is today, in the Anglophone world and more broadly in the advanced capitalist countries, that Marx is suddenly on the agenda again, almost 'trendy': the source of numerous positions in public discourse, no longer a 'bad word' associated with the ideological demonization of the USSR, and, in a sense, the main figure of theoretical resistance to the dominance of neoliberalism, a figure once again associated with the cutting edge of contemporary political thought. In such a situation, a number of key points about Karatani himself and about this work must be kept in mind.

It is probably scarcely believable to the majority of Marxists in North America and Western Europe that in the twentieth century, it could easily be argued that the most Marxist country on earth was postwar Japan. Not 'most socialist country' or 'most communist country' in the sense of forms of governance, but 'most *Marxist* country' in the sense of an intellectual culture, and certainly the most Marxist system of higher education. When Karatani entered the economics department of the University of Tokyo in the 1950s, where he studied with major figures of Marxian economics like Suzuki Kōichirō in the tradition of Uno Kōzō (about whom more shortly), the undergraduate course – 'Foundations of Economics' or 'Principles of Economics' (*Keizai genron*) – consisted of four years of intense reading, as if they were textbooks, of all three volumes of Marx's *Capital*, the *Theories of Surplus Value*, and associated works. Such a comprehensive, detailed and rigorous education in Marx's own work likely existed nowhere else at the time, and certainly not in the Soviet bloc, where the Stalin-period 'Economic Textbooks' tended to replace the works of Marx himself. It still does not exist in China, where today you are more likely to read various classics of liberalism and perhaps some 'Xi Jinping Thought' than you are to be trained up in a strict and attentive reading of Marx. In fact, throughout the twentieth century, an intensive reading of Marx tended to eventually become suspect in many of the 'actually-existing' socialist countries (although certainly not all), perhaps testifying to the dangerous power of this body of thought: if you read it too carefully, you might turn it back on us.

In many strange ways, the history of Marxism in Japan is something of which we do not yet have a clear social and political understanding, in any language, including Japanese. There is no similar precedent to this period, spanning roughly 1947 through the late 1980s, in any of the other advanced capitalist countries. The peculiarity goes further. Of course, we are speaking about the University of Tokyo, which, together with Kyoto University, form the two most prestigious sites of higher education in Japan, ever since their prewar status as two of the main 'Imperial' universities. But, in the case of the University of Tokyo economics department, we are also speaking about the essential site of training for generations of state economic planners who staffed the bureaus of the Ministry of Trade and Information (MITI), and who were, more or less, responsible for managing Japanese capitalism and its relation to the state in pursuit of the eventual and fully-achieved goal: to turn Japan into the second largest capitalist economy on earth throughout the latter half of the twentieth century. In this sense, we can even perhaps only half-jokingly assert that an education founded on the clearest and most rigorous description of a capitalist commodity economy, that of Marx, provided the essential ground for the Japanese state's runaway success as an economic force in the postwar period.

I do not mention this peculiar set of facts solely for their novelty (although it is certainly a topic that would itself benefit from extensive analysis), but to furnish an essential background to Karatani's work, his emergence as a thinker, and the theoretical landscape in which he was writing. It would be difficult to think of another country with as large a population of readers well-versed in Marx, a massive and still-successful publishing industry, and a critical space of discourse overlapping with the university, but in which it was possible to make a living by writing theoretically oriented works of literary and social criticism for a mass public audience. It is in the midst of this situation – buttressed by two other historical factors, the crisis of the New Left and the advent of a new theoretical culture in the university – that Karatani's *Marx* was first published.

Originally serialized in seven articles in the review *Gunzō* in 1973–74, Kōjin Karatani's most enduring and pioneering work in critical theory was his *Marx sono kanōsei no chūshin* (Marx: Towards the Centre of Possibility). As Karatani himself points out here in the new preface to this English edition, the first point concerning this text that must be kept in mind is its inherently interdisciplinary or even *parallax* character, to use a term that Karatani would later develop into a central concept of his thought. *Gunzō* was and is a mainstream literary periodical, not in any way a journal of the Left, nor a philosophically or theoretically specialized space of intellectual engagement. In this sense, it is all the more remarkable that a text such as the present could be published in such a venue, and bears witness to the extraordinary public nature of intellectual life in postwar Japan. Thus, the texts that make up Karatani's *Marx* were read first by a general audience, transversal to the university, and located squarely within the broad field of literary criticism.

Written at a time when the political sequences of the New Left had come to a halt under the weight of the breakdown of armed struggle, as well as the political exhaustion of competing sectarian visions of Marxism, Karatani's *Marx* laid the groundwork for major changes in Japanese intellectual life. A short text of approximately 150 pages in Japanese, it produced a new reading of Marx's work, unfamiliar to the existing Marxist discourse in Japan at the time. Since the 1920s, Marxist theory had been one of the dominant currents in Japan, so much so that one could scarcely discover a single field of the humanities and social sciences in the mid-twentieth century that had not been deeply marked by Marxism as a mode of inquiry. In this sense, Karatani's emphasis on Marx merely continued a trend that his predecessors had already inaugurated: the great postwar intellectuals, such as Uno Kōzō, Maruyama Masao, Ōtsuka Hisao, Hiromatsu Wataru and others, had all been significantly influenced by Marxism (and, in the cases of Uno and Hiromatsu, were well-known and important Marxist theorists in their own right).

However, debates within Marxism in Japan had, from the prewar period onwards, become exceedingly methodological and obscure in their fixation on textual or theoretical minutiae. The positions linked to the prewar debate on the origins of Japanese capitalism reverberated through postwar Marxism as well, constantly attempting to understand the nature of the Japanese social formation. Karatani's *Marx*, then, marked a very different moment: soon to depart for Yale at the high point of deconstruction, and in dialogue with Jacques Derrida, Paul de Man, and more, Karatani returned to the importance of Marx in Japanese intellectual life, but with a new set of theoretical tools. Semiotics, deconstruction, the reading of Marx as a *literary* thinker, and the emphasis on *Capital* as an intervention in philosophy that could be read as itself a theory of signs, produced a massive impact on Japanese intellectual life. Above all, the book represents a break – or rather is itself situated *within* a break, one might say – with the prevailing reading of Marx, dominant in 1968: that of the early Marx, a Lukácsian reading of the figure of the self-alienated labouring human. Karatani's *Marx* is a firm rebuttal to the simplistic 'theory of alienation' so beloved of the 60s generation of Marxists in Japan.

Marx sono kanōsei no chūshin began a sequence of writings of Karatani (to be followed by dozens of further works, including among others *Investigations I* and *II*, *Introspection and Retrospection*) that were crucial in the development of critical theory in Japan. Karatani, along with his compatriot Akira Asada, would go on to essentially produce a parallel development in Japan to what had been institutionalized in the United States as 'French theory', and often referred to as 'new academism' in Japan. But Karatani's *Marx* is unique in this sense, not only because of its importance in modern Japanese intellectual history after the moment of 1968, but also because the reading of Marx that Karatani debuts in this text will go on to form the basis of his 'transcritical' work that would culminate decades later in texts such as *Architecture as Metaphor*, *Transcritique* and *The Structure of World History*. All of these texts have now made an increasing impact in the English-speaking world, seen as an important and singular intervention in critical theory and Marxist thought.

The translation of *Marx sono kanōsei no chūshin* in this sense fills a void: both to make clear the origins of Karatani's own work on Marx, but also to show its *groundwork*, as it were. It is in this text that Karatani's peculiar blend of influences (Marx, mathematics, formal and Saussurean linguistics, anthropology, literary analysis, geometry, and more) is concatenated together for the first time, and thus constitutes a crucial text in our understanding of Karatani's thought: it is also his most singular and sustained engagement directly with Marx in his body of work.

In the initial lines of the present work, Karatani writes:

> To deal with a thinker is to deal with his or her work. This may seem an obvious point, but in fact it is not. For example, in order to consider Marx, one should intensively read *Capital*. But people instead pass through certain external ideologies such as historical materialism or dialectical materialism, and

merely read *Capital* in order to confirm these ideological presuppositions. This is not reading. What I mean by reading a work is rather: to read neither with the presupposition of philosophical concerns external to the work itself nor authorial intention.

For Karatani, the act of reading, the politics of reading, consist in reading towards *the centre of possibility* expressed in the given text, and it is precisely this centre of possibility that we should affirm as the analytical core of our own reading of his project, a project devoted above all to the paradoxical explication of capital's structures and the heretical creation of concepts for its overcoming, rather than to the canonical enforcement of academic genealogies and filiations. In contrast to Hiromatsu Wataru's imposing *Shihonron no tetsugaku* (The Philosophy of *Capital*),[1] published the same year (1974) as Karatani's *Marx* began serialization, Karatani writes in a style that is deceptively simple and remarkably clear. A consistent feature of his work for decades, this speaks not only to the clarity of his thought but to his consciousness as a public intellectual.

In a sense, Karatani's text – written as a public intervention – contains little that would help the reader situate its position genealogically, with one exception. Karatani affords a crucial place to the thought of one figure in Marxist theoretical analysis from whom he absorbed a crucial and general conceptual problem. The thinker is Uno Kōzō (1897–1977), and the problem, in the broadest possible terms, is the relationship of capital to its *outside*, as it were. Uno, who would go on to become one of the most dominant figures in Marxist theoretical research in Japan, and indeed one of the most famous thinkers of Marx's value theory worldwide,[2] was educated at

---

[1] On Hiromatsu, see the important recent work of Watanabe Yasuhiko, *Hiromatsu Wataru no shisō: Naizai no dainamizumu* (Tokyo: Misuzu Shobō, 2018).

[2] In English, see Thomas T. Sekine's translation, *Principles of*

Tokyo University.³ He left Japan to study abroad in Berlin from 1922–24, where he was accompanied by his long-time friend Sakisaka Itsurō, later the editor of the Kaizōsha edition of the *Marx–Engels Collected Works* – the first in the world in any language – and leader of the Japan Socialist Party following the war. (Incidentally, the so-called 'Weimar hyperinflation' of this period meant that with the favourable exchange rate, the Japanese Ministry of Education stipends for overseas researchers and students in Germany were worth a small fortune, and, in an interesting historical irony, it was this government money that allowed Sakisaka and other Marxist students to collect the materials that would compose the Collected Works and other original Marxian sources). Uno returned to Japan in 1924 (incidentally, on the same boat as the early Japan Communist Party leader Fukumoto Kazuo),⁴ where he began to teach, first at Tohoku University until 1938, when he was arrested on suspicion of his political stance. From this moment until the end of the war, Uno was forced to remain outside academic life, working in the statistics bureau of the Japanese External Trade Organization, followed by the Economic Research Institute of the Mitsubishi corporation. After the war, in 1946, he was reappointed as full professor in the department of economics at Tokyo University, and immediately released almost a decade of theoretical work that had been impossible to publish

---

Political Economy: Theory of a Purely Capitalist Society (Hemel Hempstead: Harvester Press, 1980). In Japanese, see Uno's collected works in *UKC*, ten vols + one supplemental (Tokyo: Iwanami Shoten, 1973).

3 This section draws from my longer consideration of Uno in Gavin Walker, 'The Absent Body of Labour Power: Uno Kōzō's Logic of Capital', in *Historical Materialism*, vol. 21, no. 4, Autumn 2013 (Leiden: Brill, 2013), 1-34, and its extension in *The Sublime Perversion of Capital* (Durham: Duke University Press, 2016).

4 On this episode and on his time in Berlin, see Uno Kōzō, *Shihonron gojūnen* (Fifty Years with *Capital*), vol. 1 (Tokyo: Hōsei University Press, 1970), 184-252.

under the fascist system – *Theory of Value* (*Kachiron*, 1947), *Prolegomena to the Agrarian Question* (*Nōgyō mondai joron*, 1947), *Introduction to 'Capital'* (*Shihonron nyūmon*, 1948), and the first series of articles that would later form his two-volume *Principles of Political Economy* (*Keizai genron*, 1950).

Uno is best known for his reschematization and reformulation of Marx's economic thought, exemplified by *Capital*, into a highly formalized, purified system designed to create a 'scientific' political economy on par with the other social sciences coming to the fore in the immediate postwar period, and it is this work that should be seen as a clear background to Karatani's text. The most basic distinguishing methodological feature of Uno's system, the theory of three levels of analysis or *sandankairon*, is a tripartite division of the practice of theory, and represents an effort to construct a general economic meta-epistemology capable of dealing with the primary contradictions of not only the conjuncture of Japanese capitalism (and the constant debate within Japanese Marxism on its origins and development), but also the theoretical concerns internal to Marxian economics. Structurally, Uno proposes three levels of analysis: 1) the level of pure theory or 'principles' (*genriron*), the logic of capital made rigorously theorizable by allowing its tendency to finally commodify itself, forming a pure interiority expressed as a thought-experiment; 2) the level of the theory of stages (*dankairon*), wherein the logic of a pure capitalism encounters its own necessity to develop *historically* and *in the world*, through specific regimes of accumulation – liberalist, mercantilist, imperialist; and 3) the level of analysis of the contemporary situation or conjuncture (*genjō bunseki*).

What this division accomplishes in its separation of a level of 'pure theory' or 'principles' is an attempt to draw closer to the possibility of a Marxist logic – Uno often emphasized the importance of understanding Lenin's famous argument in the *Philosophical Notebooks* that 'If Marx did not leave behind him a *"Logic"* [with a capital letter], he did leave the *logic* of *Capital*.⁵ By attempting to develop to the furthest extent possible the *Logic* inherent in *Capital*, Uno also exposed or ran up against the limits of this logic, the historical contamination that is always paradoxically included in the thought-experiment of a 'purely capitalist society'. Although most work on Uno over the last fifty years has focused on his methodology in terms of this tripartite division of theoretical practice, we might rather say that the essence or truly critical moment in Uno's work lies elsewhere, in a short phrase that he considered the 'nucleus' or theoretical centre of his work, one that is constantly returning in his writing to undermine the smooth or 'pure' logic of *Capital*, or rather, one that expresses the *logical* problem for the dynamics of capitalism around the labour power commodity.

On a worldwide level, analysis of Uno's work has almost always agreed on its supposedly 'pure' character – that is, he is widely considered the most esoteric, purely theoretical, excessively formalistic and scholastic figure in the Marxian analysis of value; but I argue that this is not at all the case. In itself, Uno's assertion that Marx's work must be reconstructed as a theory of principle – a theory of a relatively *pure* capitalism or one that has developed in the direction of the principles of the capital-relation itself – is not particularly controversial. After all, Marx himself declared that the capitalism under analysis in *Capital* was not exactly synonymous with English capitalist development *as such* but rather constituted an 'ideal average' of the capitalist mode of production:

> In our description of how production relations are converted into entities and rendered independent in relation to the agents of production, we leave aside the manner in which the interrelations, due to the world market, its conjunctures, movements

---

5 V. I. Lenin, *Collected Works*, 4th Edition, vol. 38 (Moscow: Progress Publishers, 1976), 317. See on this point Uno Kōzō, *Shihonron to shakaishugi* in *UKC*, vol. 10, in particular pp. 4–7.

of market prices, periods of credit, industrial and commercial cycles, alternations of prosperity and crisis, appear to them as overwhelming natural laws that irresistibly enforce their will over them, and confront them as blind necessity. We leave this aside because the actual movement of competition belongs beyond our scope, and we need present *only the inner organisation of the capitalist mode of production, in its ideal average, as it were* [*nur die innere Organisation der kapitalistischen Produktionsweise, sozusagen in ihrem idealen Durchschnitt*].[6]

In attempting to treat as much as possible the inner dynamics of this ideal 'average' or 'cross-section' (*Durchschnitt*) of capital's *logical drive*, Uno makes a wager on the possibility of a certain excessive formalism as the only means available to us to 'express' the abstraction of the circuit-process of capital. But, in the most theoretically innovative aspect of his work, he always undercuts or *contaminates* the purity of this circuit by drawing our attention to one decisive phrase that concentrates within it the density of politics. This is what Uno referred to with his famous and enigmatic phrase 'the *impasse* or *(im)possibility* of the commodification of labour power' (*rōdōryoku shōhinka no 'muri'*).[7] What he means by this simply – although it is not at all a 'simple' point – is that the starting-point of the systematic logic of political economy must always 'suppose' (*setzen*) something entirely irrational as

---

[6] Marx, *Das Kapital*, Bd. 3 in *MEW*, Bd. 25, 839; Marx, *Capital*, vol. 3 in *MECW*, vol. 37, 818. Translation modified.

[7] This term '*muri*' is a commonplace and everyday expression in conversational Japanese. It can be used to indicate that something is impossible, improbable, unlikely, etc., as well as an injunction to not 'overdo it' or 'do something to excess', to 'strain oneself', or 'go over the top'. Numerous translations of it are possible: impossibility, (im)possibility, excess, irrationality, impasse and so forth. As we will see, Uno in no way argues that this *muri* is completely impossible, rather it is a limit, but one that is constantly present, constantly 'passing through'. In general on this point, see Gavin Walker, *The Sublime Perversion of Capital*.

the ground of the rationality of the historical process, which will then be 'retrojected' back onto the moment of origin in order to once again 'presuppose' (*voraussetzen*) it *as if it were rational*. Uno once wrote:

> A commodity economy inherently possesses an impossibility or impasse (*muri*) insofar as it treats relations among human beings as relations among things, but it is paradoxically the fact that this impossibility (*muri*) has developed as a form capable of ordering the totality of society that in turn renders possible our own theoretical systematisation of its motion.[8]

In turn, in the present text, Karatani writes:

> In capitalist society, labour power becomes a commodity. Strictly speaking, it is not labour power that becomes a commodity, but the concept of labour power itself – distinct from labour – is something that already comes from the analysis of the commodity form. That labour power could be a commodity is nothing more than a tautology; what is crucial is that the owner of labour power appeared *historically*.

Often accused of prioritizing exchange over the sphere of production, Karatani is simply extending and developing in part an insight that stems from Marx himself and that intervenes in a sense well before such a division could be enacted. 'Commodities', Marx reminds us, 'cannot themselves go to market and perform exchanges in their own right. We must, therefore, have recourse to their guardians (*Hütern*), who are the possessors of commodities (*Warenbesitzern*).'[9] This point is crucial for us to consider when we attempt to take up one of the essential points of Karatani's work: his emphasis on the set of questions contained not strictly within the sphere of production, but those contained as it were, in the parallax

---

[8] Uno, 'Keizaigaku ni okeru ronshō to jisshō' in *UKC*, vol. 4, 19.
[9] Marx, *Das Kapital*, Bd 1 in *MEW*, Bd 23: 99; Marx, *Capital*, vol. 1 in *MECW*, vol. 35: 94.

between circulation and production. In order to understand the position of the seller and buyer of labour power in the market, we require, in certain senses, a reversal of the typical schema through which we read Marx. We often presuppose or allow ourselves to imagine a hierarchy of spheres, in which the circulation-surface is subtended by the 'hidden abode of production'. But this too can be a merely mystifying point unless we consider the problem of what is given or what must be *presupposed* in the production process: precisely the availability of labour power, that archi-commodity at the origin of the entire social landscape, without which we remain in a process of infinite referral between instances to seal the basic gap that it represents. It is precisely for this reason that we must remember Marx's point: 'It is ... impossible for capital to be produced by circulation, and it is equally impossible for it to originate apart from circulation. It must have its origin both in circulation and yet not in circulation.'[10]

Karatani's intervention is not only an intervention into the logic of capital, it is an intervention in history, and in politics, one that in some sense also gave way to the rebirth of Marxist theoretical analysis in the Japanese situation, now linked to a whole anti-humanist tradition that was being developed globally through the 70s. In the first afterword, written in 1978, to the republished Japanese edition of *Marx sono kanōsei no chūshin*, Karatani speaks extensively of the background to this work: 'Insofar as every author writes within a language and a logic, every author possesses a unique system. But the richness of a work exists insofar as there is a system that the author cannot control *within* the systematic structure that the author is consciously in control of.'[11] The same can be said for Karatani's text itself, and as a thinker of genuinely rigorous consistency – remarkable over a period of nearly fifty

---

10 Marx, *Capital*, vol. 1 in *MECW*, vol. 35 (New York: International Publishers, 1996), 165–6.

11 Karatani, *Marx sono kanōsei no chūshin* (1978), Afterword.

years of public writing and theoretical work – he would surely agree. In the present text, he writes:

> What I refuse is the historicist fiction of Marx's conceptual development, from the dissertation to *Capital*. If *Capital* didn't exist, who would even bother reading back to Marx's dissertation? The early Marx is not the origin of *Capital*, but its result. Even the originality of this dissertation first becomes clear, not in relation to its meaning within the temporal context of its writing, but rather within the reading of *Capital*.

We, too, might refuse the 'historicist fiction' that would see the present text as a secret 'origin' for Karatani's work. In some sense, it is rather the reverse: Karatani's later work has now given us a new vantage point from which to read and re-read the present work.

In returning to a textually centred reading of Marx, Karatani burrows into the inner contradictions and the inner structure of *Capital* as a text, but also of capital as a concept. Here, in the aftermath of the fantasies of the full plenitude of the subjective political intervention that characterized the end of '68, Karatani places the emphasis squarely on the side of capital, following Marx in his point that 'the very necessity of *general political action* affords the proof that in its merely economic action capital is the stronger side.'[12] In recent years, Karatani has come to address principally what he calls the Borromean knot of 'capital-nation-state', and particularly the supplementary relationship that capital requires to sustain its pretence of operating as a purely self-contained cycle, reminding us of the essential madness of capital and its corresponding system of thought. It is precisely in this sense of capital's demented undercurrent, covered over or erased by its two impossibilities in the so-called primitive accumulation and the commodification of labour power, that the two polarities are in a constant

---

12 Marx, *Value, Price and Profit*, in *MECW*, vol. 20, 146.

inversion or reversal into each, whereby the logical topology of the irrational commodification of labour power in the circulation process (annulled by being covered over in the form of money) reappears in the production process as the absurdity, madness, violence, and exteriority of the historical cartography of the process of primitive accumulation. This entire cycle furnishes us with the basic problem of the supplement, in the form of the origin that erases itself as an origin, a problem that is not overcome, but merely *passed through* or *traversed* through the gift, whereby what cannot ever be said to be purely given must be there at the commencement for the entire cycle to operate. In turn, it is Karatani's emphasis on the question of modes of exchange – his recent development, but one that can surely be connected with the present text – within the logico-historical dynamics of capital that might lead us directly to a new direction of analysis capable of understanding how the dynamics of *commodification* of that which cannot strictly be commodified – labour power and land – can *pass through* our social life *as if* they could be smoothly assumed, so that this impossible or excessive 'gift' of capital is refigured in the final form of *reification*, a reification in which capital in the end reifies itself.

Karatani's triangular structure of capital-nation-state is also an emphasis on how each of these instances of the trinity serve temporarily as forces of mediation for each other: the nation mediating capital's schema of buyer and seller of labour power, presupposed in the sphere of circulation, the state mediating the nation's drive for communal integration through citizenship systems and policy initiatives in the gap between prosperity and recession. By focusing on the centrality of capital's supplementarity – its originary supplemental role – Karatani also opens up for us another possible thinking of the subject in capitalist society, the *political* subject, after and in the wake of 1968. In precisely the place where the hole or wound of commodity-economic rationality lies, the structure of sentiment, but also the openness of practice remains. This is the domain of the political, of class struggle as such, a point where the Borromean knot of these three figures Capital-Nation-State are knotted together. Rather than reveal our stasis, our enclosure into permanent capture, Karatani's emphasis on the sphere of circulation instead shows us the place of the primacy of politics, the possibilities of a genuinely political response to the subsumptive force of capitalist society. Karatani's *Marx* is itself a text whose lessons, arranged after the end of the last great global revolutionary surge of the late 60s, remain full of possibilities, possibilities that lead us into the centre of our political condition today.

Preface to the English Edition

This book is a piece of literary criticism that I originally wrote in 1973 and serialized in a monthly literary periodical. However, the fact that I undertook the present work within the field of criticism was by no means normal or expected within the Japanese situation. Rather, it was probably the first time that such critical work could be published in a literary magazine alongside short stories and serialized novels. Yet, at the same time, it might also be said that this type of work was impossible to publish somewhere else – for example, in specialist journals of philosophy or the social sciences. In that sense, the present work is without question a work of literary criticism.

In Japan, the New Left movement emerged in the second half of the 1950s. We can say that it was influenced by the critique of Stalinism that accompanied the Hungarian revolt, but we can also relate its emergence to the beginnings of the rapid economic growth that was occurring at the same time in Japan. Suddenly a set of circumstances that could not be explained by the theoretical framework of the existing Left had emerged, for example, the phenomena of mass society and consumer society. The New Left movement which prospered alongside this development brought about a loss of authority for the Japan Communist Party (which had been strong until that point), through the nationwide political struggles that accompanied the 1960 revisions to the US–Japan Joint Security Treaty (often abbreviated *Anpō*). In a sense, what occurred in 1968 in Europe and North America occurred already in Japan at this moment. I entered Tokyo University in the year 1960 and participated in what we called the '*Anpō*

Struggle'. However, what made me reflect on the theoretical questions of the Left came later – it came, in fact, after this struggle ended in failure.

The theoretical work of the New Left which emerged in the late 1950s can be divided into three general trends, all derived from the work of Marx. The first turned towards the early Marx and the theory of alienation, represented most clearly by the literary critic and poet Yoshimoto Taka'aki (1924–2012). The second, what we might call the reconstruction of historical materialism through a re-reading that attempted to overcome the early Marx, was best represented in the figure of the philosopher Hiromatsu Wataru (1933–1994). The third, which sought to rediscover Marx's specificity in the text of *Capital*, can be represented by the political economist Uno Kōzō (1897–1977).

I was influenced by all three of these figures. For example, what drew me to literary criticism in the first place was the influence of Yoshimoto Taka'aki. On the one hand, what led me to reject the theoretical work of the early Marx on which Yoshimoto had relied so much, was precisely the influence of Hiromatsu Wataru. He provided textual proof that Engels had pre-empted the process that Althusser, for instance, referred to as Marx's 'epistemological break'. Yet, on the other hand, the greatest influence on me by far came from Uno Kōzō's theoretical work in political economy.

In Uno's conception, while *Capital* constituted the 'guiding thread' of historical materialism, it was written with a differing perspective and methodological orientation. Historical materialism views the history of social formations from the economic base of modes of production (forces of production and relations of production). In contrast, *Capital* explicates the capitalist economic system by beginning from commodity exchange and disclosing the process by which it comes to compose and regulate the relations of production *as capital*. Although these two modes of thinking are heterogeneous to each other, the majority of Marxist theorists ignored the clear differential between them and tried to somehow produce an articulation between these two perspectives. Uno Kōzō, however, rigorously distinguished them, insisting on *Capital* as 'science' and historical materialism as 'ideology', although this ideology remained necessary as a 'guiding thread'.

Moreover, Uno's reading of *Capital* itself was creative and original. In general, *Capital* was treated as a text in which the labour theory of value had been inherited from the classical political economy of Smith and Ricardo, but for Uno, *Capital* focused on exchange rather than production, and, in this sense, he emphasized precisely that capital itself was, in essence, merchant capital. I agreed with Uno's thought, and soon entered the economics department of the University of Tokyo. Although Uno himself had already retired by this point, I encountered there numerous professors who belonged to the Uno School. But, before long, I lost interest in economics; after graduating, I turned towards literature and became a critic. Nevertheless, I certainly had not lost my interest in Marx's *Capital*, rather, I was simply uninterested in treating it as an economist.

From my perspective, I saw the capitalist economy as disclosed in *Capital* not as something material but as an ideal superstructure founded on credit, something born not from the sphere of production but rather from the enigma of exchange. Marx famously stated that exchange began from the interval or intercourse between one community and another. But, in such circumstances, where does this 'power' that seems to secure and guarantee exchange with an unknown, uncanny other come from? Marx discovered it in the form of the *fetish* that adheres to things. In this sense, I understood *Capital* as a work depicting the process by which the fetish (commodity) develops into Mammon (capital) – but to read *Capital* in this way was impossible within the sphere of economics proper, and equally impossible within the field of philosophy.

Marx writes: 'A commodity seems at first glance to be a self-evident, trivial thing. The analysis of it yields the insight that it is a very vexatious thing, full of metaphysical subtlety and theological perversities.'[1] In other words, *Capital* itself is not a text that simply treats metaphysical or theological questions, but one that attempts to draw them out from within this 'self-evident, trivial thing' called the commodity. I believed that, in order to theorize this precise problem, it was only possible do so within literary criticism. However, I only began this project in 1973, after I had already published two earlier books as a literary critic. And there was another reason that I specifically wrote a text on Marx at that particular time: it was the very moment at which the New Left movements of the end of the 1960s had failed, and the voices that loudly proclaimed the 'end of Marxism' were becoming more and more hegemonic. This was not new to me, since similar voices had already been heard at the beginning of the 1960s, precisely the situation within which I began to read *Capital* voraciously.

Thus, *Marx: Towards the Centre of Possibility* was an attempt to read *Capital* from the perspective of literary criticism. What I called here 'the centre of possibility' indicates a form of meaning or signification that is there despite not being explicitly specified in the text. In other words, it exists more in the 'margins' than in the actual 'centre', a mode of seeing and reading that I learned from the critical writings of Paul Valéry. But we can also discover this mode in Marx's own words. For example, in 1858, he writes the following to Ferdinand Lassalle, with regard to his own doctoral dissertation, *The Difference Between the Democritean and Epicurean Philosophy of Nature*:

> I am all the more aware of the difficulties you had to surmount in this work in that about 18 years ago I myself attempted a similar work on a far easier philosopher, Epicurus – namely

---

[1] Marx, *Capital*, vol. 1 (first German edition).

the portrayal of a complete system from fragments, a system which I am convinced, by the by, was – as with Heraclitus – only *implicitly* present in his work, not consciously as a system. Even in the case of philosophers who give systematic form to their work, Spinoza for instance, the true inner structure of the system is quite unlike the form in which it was consciously presented by him.[2]

I tried to conceive of Marx's 'system' in precisely the same way. For example, *Capital* was written to an extent on the basis of Hegel's logical system, but its 'true inner structure' is 'quite unlike the form in which it was consciously presented'. I attempted to see the economic problems detailed in *Capital* from an entirely different viewpoint by trying to theorize commodity exchange from the perspective of linguistic exchange, or communication. At the time, I discovered a form of thought that resembled that of Marx in the theoretical linguistics of Saussure.

In his theory of the value-form at the outset of *Capital*, Marx grasped the value of the commodity within a relational system of commodities. In the same way, Saussure took language (*langue*) to be a synchronic, differential system of signifiers: the meaning of one word is determined in relation to words outside it. Just by changing one element within a synchronic system, it becomes an entirely different system. Thus, what we see as the continual diachronic transformation of language is in fact a discontinuous process of transformation from one synchronic system to another. This is more or less the foundational insight of what came to be called 'structuralism'. However, what struck me above all in the work of Saussure was that he theorized precisely the exchange or communication that takes place in the interval between multiple systems.

For example, Saussure argued that if a word in one system is translated into another system, while its 'meaning' might be the same, it will possess a different 'value' insofar as its relation

---

[2] Marx, letter of 31 May 1858 to Lasalle in *MECW*, vol. 40, 316.

to other words will itself differ. From this point I took a set of clues as to the theorization of surplus value. In other words, we might as well say that surplus value constitutes a differential that emerges from the exchange between different systems. Classical political economy described merchant capital as the process of buying cheap and selling dear. However, it is not the case that merchants practise unequal exchange. A thing may be cheap within one synchronic system, and expensive in another. Although each thing itself emerged from equal exchange within each system, a differential between them is born from exchange. We cannot say that the merchants who acquired this differential were unjust or unfair. Generally speaking, this differential was born in the trade between territories remote from each other.

Adam Smith criticized merchant capital but endorsed the profits gained from industrial capital, on the basis that they were earned through equal exchange. Yet industrial capital also makes profits from the differential generated through this very 'equal exchange' itself. In other words, it gains surplus value from the differential of purchasing labour power in the labour market and selling what the labourer is forced to produce on the open market. Both merchant capital and industrial capital are based on equal exchange. The difference lies in the following point: in the case of merchant capital, the differential comes from the spatial difference between synchronic systems, while in the case of industrial capital, it comes from the temporal differentiation between synchronic systems. It is the differentiation of value systems on the basis of technical innovation, and it is for this reason that industrial capital leads towards ceaseless technical development. Obviously, capital is indifferent to the diverse ways it can gain surplus value and thereby increase itself; this is precisely why capital itself is essentially merchant capital, and why Marx is able to define the accumulation of capital with the general M–C–M' formula.

PREFACE TO THE ENGLISH EDITION

I came to the above understanding through the various hints I took from Saussurean linguistics. But what I later recognized is that there was a basis beyond mere analogy for the introduction of Saussure into the reading of *Capital* that I undertook in the present work. Saussure himself began to conceive of synchronic systems in language by means of the analogy with economics, and specifically with the general equilibrium theory of the Swiss economist Léon Walras. Walras rejected the classical labour theory of value, conceiving of value from the perspective of marginal utility, in other words, the theory of the neoclassical school. This appears, at first glance, to be in direct opposition to *Capital*, but it is not at all the case. As Volume 3 demonstrates, Marx conceived of prices of production separately from labour values, and in his theory of rent posited the importance of marginal costs, following Ricardo, in opposition to the theory of equilibrium of classical political economy. In terms of the theory of rent, Ricardo clearly belonged to classical political economy, but, in contrast to the classical school's concept of 'equilibrium', he brought in the concept of the 'marginal'. There is an important relation here as well to Marx's work of the 1870s and after on questions of differential calculus (see the *Mathematical Manuscripts*).[3] In this sense, at the same historical moment, Marx shared a certain *problématique* with Menger, Walras, and the 'Marginal Revolution'.

To put it in terms of economics, Saussure's thought not only overcame that of the classical school, but also that of the neoclassical. He did not just develop the notion of synchronic systems as a concept; he attempted to theorize the exchange (communication) between differing systems. In turn, Marx's critique of political economy also implies not only a critique of classical political economy, but of the neoclassical school as well. In my view, this is precisely because Marx attempted

---

3 Marx, *Mathematical Manuscripts* (London: New Park Publications, 1983).

to think the problems of a capitalist economy from the standpoint of exchange.

Since the original publication of *Marx: Towards the Centre of Possibility* in 1973, I have attempted to fundamentally rethink the theoretical problem, in the broadest sense, of the exchange or communication with the other. This theoretical project passed from linguistics itself to the logical foundations of mathematics, and then to my philosophical *Investigations*.[4] During this period, I did not really deal with or theoretically treat the work of Marx. When I started to work on Marx again, it was the beginning of the 1990s: the Soviet Union had imploded, and the US–Soviet Cold War period had come to an end. Around the world, there were loud proclamations about 'the end of history' and 'the end of Marxism'. In the years to follow, historical materialism was not refuted, but it lost its authority. If we consider this, we might say that the moment when I began to write about Marx initially (1973) was precisely a moment of Marxism's downfall, and the 1990s were much the same.

For historical materialism, the forces of production and the relations of production constitute the base, which determines the ideational-political superstructure. However, in this type of economic determinism, there is no genuine scope to elucidate the 'superstructural' role of the state, of religion, and so forth. The state or religion, however, possess a power or force that can be neither explained nor resolved by means of the economic base. Here, no matter how much the economic base is taken to be determinant for the ideational-political superstructure, it comes to be generally recognized as possessing a relative autonomy. Yet, as soon as we admit this, the economic base's determining function is perhaps not negated, but certainly disappears as a point of emphasis. Thus, in some

---

4 [Trans.] Karatani's influential *Investigations I* and *II* (*Tankyū I, II*) were published in 1986 and 1989.

sense, the conception of the economic base has been in reality totally forgotten.

Right at the moment of the 1990s, I again took up the questions of historical materialism. I attempted to discover the 'economic base' of the historical social formation not in the sphere of production, but in exchange. In this sense, exchange is not something secondary to or derivative of production, but rather its prior condition of possibility. Already, in *Marx: Towards the Centre of Possibility*, I had theorized this expanded conception of exchange. However, even if the book touched on the realm of linguistics, I did not go beyond a thinking of the economic in its narrow sense. It was in the 1990s that I first came to locate the problem of exchange in matters that are not usually considered to be forms of exchange themselves.

Marcel Mauss saw in the exchange of gifts and reciprocity the basis of clan society. I referred to this as 'mode of exchange A', the introduction of the power that constructs community. Similarly, I theorized the formation of the state in terms of voluntary surrender and protection, or taxation and redistribution, what I called mode of exchange B. This is precisely where the state's power – different from military force – comes from. And I referred to the sphere of ordinary commodity exchange as mode of exchange C, in a sense, the origin of the power of money.

To these three modes, we can add mode of exchange D, which attempts to sublate the others, like the power of God, which manifested in the form of universal religion in the age of the ancient empires. D is local, something that always remained within the later social formation; in the second half of the nineteenth century, it appeared in our world as communism. In his later years, Marx stressed the importance of Lewis Henry Morgan's *Ancient Society*, arguing that communism was nothing other than 'the return of modern society to a higher form of the most archaic type – collective production and appropriation'.[5] To rephrase it, mode of exchange D is the return of mode of exchange A 'in a higher form'.

Historically speaking, the social formation is the articulation of multiple modes of exchange. In primitive society, mode of exchange A is dominant. What we must be careful to point out is that, even at this stage, modes of exchange B and C already exist in nascent form. If B becomes dominant, the state is formed. In such a moment, however, A is not eliminated, but continues to exist in the form of the agrarian community subjugated by the force of the state and the landowner. On the other hand, C is expanded by means of the development of B. In other words, at the stage of the formation of multiple territorial states, the money economy emerged. In the ancient world empires, A and C are combined under the dominance of B.

Mode of exchange C rose to prominence in the social formation with the appearance of industrial capital, and this is precisely the process Marx sought to explicate in *Capital*. However, from the perspective of modes of exchange, we need to be careful to emphasize that, when industrial capital emerged, it also caused a transformation of the social formation as a whole, and as a combination of all of the modes of exchange. That is, A and B did not diminish, but were altered in form by the dominance of C. B took the form of the bourgeois state, while A formed the 'imagined community' of the nation. To put it simply in my terms, this constituted the triadic structure of capital-nation-state.

At the end of the 1990s, I proposed the above mode of analysis in my *Transcritique: On Kant and Marx*. Once again, I did this by means of a specific way of reading the texts of Marx and Kant, which is to say I took a more or less literary-critical stance, and once again published it for the first time in a literary magazine in serial form. Subsequently I discarded

---

5 Marx, 'Letter to Vera Zasulich', in *MECW*, vol. 24.

this stance and began a process of systematically constructing my theoretical work as a whole. In fact, I abandoned literary criticism completely. In a sense, you could say that what I have attempted to do since that moment is to reconstruct *Capital* as a 'guiding thread', this time with its economic base not in modes of production, but in modes of exchange. The process culminated in *The Structure of World History*.[6] In the present work, I speak from an understanding that might be seen to differ from that of Marx. But I would rather think that in fact, what I discovered there was precisely 'the centre of possibility' in Marx.

Tokyo, April 2019

---

6 Kōjin Karatani, *The Structure of World History*, trans. Michael Bourdaghs (Durham: Duke University Press, 2014).

> Mankind inevitably sets itself only such tasks as it is able to solve.[1]
> – Marx

> Man cannot discover himself by increasing his perception, but only through the tasks he defines for himself.[2]
> – Malraux

> Essential thinkers always say the Same.[3]
> – Heidegger

---

1 Karl Marx, 'Preface' to *A Contribution to the Critique of Political Economy*, in *Marx–Engels Collected Works* (hereafter *MECW*), vol. 29, 263.

2 André Malraux, *Man's Fate* [*La condition humaine*], trans. H. M. Chevalier (New York: Vintage, 1990).

3 Martin Heidegger, 'Letter on Humanism', in *Pathmarks*, ed. W. McNeill (Cambridge: Cambridge University Press, 1998), 275.

Chapter One

1

To deal with a thinker is to deal with his or her work. This may seem an obvious point, but, in fact, it is not. For example, in order to consider Marx, one should intensively read *Capital*. But people instead pass through certain external ideologies such as historical materialism or dialectical materialism, and merely read *Capital* in order to confirm these ideological presuppositions. This is not reading. What I mean by reading a work is, rather, to read neither with the presupposition of philosophies external to the work itself nor authorial intention. *Capital: A Critique of Political Economy* is already widely considered a 'classic' in the history of political economy. This indicates two things. On the one hand, it suggests that *Capital* itself, along with the conceptual world and knowledge that it examines, is antiquated and out of date; on the other hand, as with the experience of reading Epicurus or Spinoza, reading the 'classics' is precisely already an experience of ignoring all external appearances, and, instead, reading toward the centre of possibility contained in the text.

In his letter of 31 May 1858 to Ferdinand Lassalle, Marx states the following:

> During this time of tribulation I carefully perused your *Heraclitus*. Your reconstruction of the system from the scattered fragments I regard as brilliant, nor was I any less impressed by the perspicacity of your polemic. ... I am all the more aware of the difficulties you had to surmount in this work in that about

18 years ago I myself attempted a similar work on a far easier philosopher, Epicurus – namely the portrayal of a complete system from fragments, a system which I am convinced, by the by, was – as with Heraclitus – only *implicitly* present in his work, not consciously as a system. Even in the case of philosophers who give systematic form to their work, Spinoza for instance, the true inner structure of the system is quite unlike the form in which it was consciously presented by him.[1]

Marx's insight is by no means applicable solely to thinkers of the past. What he accomplished in his work on *Capital* was precisely a critique of the conscious systematization of capitalist society (classical political economy), and a simultaneous illumination of the 'inner structure of the capitalist mode of production'. We might say that, behind this belief of Marx's, lay a certain sense that no one else had yet conceived of the problem in quite this way.

But we will take up this problem at a later moment. What we must emphasize for now is the fact that the above words of Marx are equally applicable to his own work. As he states, it is meaningless to distinguish a given thinker's work in terms of its appearance of systematicity or fragmentation. All anti-systematic thinkers are systematic in an internal sense, and if not, are not essential thinkers, that is, they do not think *radically* – at the root of things.

Let us take, for example, someone like Montaigne, who is seen as a representative anti-systematic thinker. We cannot unify and consolidate all that Montaigne states. In his thought there is an Epicurean moment, a Stoic moment, and a sort of Pascalian Christianity, yet he never gives the impression of a mere jumble of influences. If we are to read the *Essays* carefully, we find that a kind of principle resides there, or a function of the spirit that appears as a principle. What never ceases to remain fresh in the *Essays* is not its anti-systematicity or its

---

[1] Marx, letter of 31 May 1858 to Lassalle in *MECW*, vol. 40, 316.

tendency towards contradiction, but, rather, the fact that at its base is Montaigne's attempt to view every contradiction with new eyes. Thus, the fragmentary form of his thought is rather like a continuous protest against a transparent meaning, a meaning that would exceed the text.

He states as follows:

> I propose a life ordinary and without lustre: 'tis all one; all moral philosophy may as well be applied to a common and private life, as to one of richer composition: every man carries the entire form of the human condition. Authors communicate themselves to the people by some especial and extrinsic mark; *I, the first of any*, by my universal being; as Michel de Montaigne, not as a grammarian, a poet, or a lawyer. If the world find fault that I speak too much of myself, I find fault that they do not so much as think of themselves.[2]

This is an ironic statement: in fact, Montaigne is neither writing nor thinking of his so-called 'self' at all. Rather, he states, the people only think of themselves. When Montaigne says, 'I, the first of any', he is speaking of the *first* discovery of the conviction that this thing called 'I' or 'the self' can become the subject. In contrast to authors up to this point, Montaigne is simply saying: you all, as philosophers and poets, may speak of the human being, of the spirit, and so on, but in fact you're not yet speaking of anything at all. I'm tired of all explanation, determination, interpretation. I will instead speak – with neither presupposition nor hesitation – of this absolutely commonplace, yet strange and mysterious thing called 'I'.

What Montaigne here depicts is not a series of former ideas concerning 'the human', but rather what we might call its inner structure. All ideas of 'the human' are destroyed by Montaigne. But this was no threat to him, because he fundamentally believes that the figure of 'the human' discovered by

---

[2] Michel de Montaigne, *Selected Essays*, ed. W. C. Hazlitt (New York: Dover, 2011), 172.

religion and philosophy is merely the signified, and at its base is the strange signifier of the 'I'. In other words, for Montaigne there is an 'I' that is neither the subject nor self-consciousness, but, conversely, is the source from which these emerge. This is not the so-called 'self', but rather the very text he quotes.

Marx writes as follows in the first edition of *Capital*:

> A commodity seems at first glance to be a self-evident, trivial thing. The analysis of it yields the insight that it is a very vexatious thing, full of metaphysical subtlety and theological perversities.[3]

Previous political economists had already formulated the system of political economy on the basis of categorical arrangements derived from what existed before their eyes. It is possible to say that Marx inherited these various categories and critically reconstructed them, but the capacity to see the most simple and commonplace commodity as 'full of metaphysical subtlety and theological perversities' was in no way already an aspect of the existing political economy. All economists – and economists in particular – merely passed through this simple thing as if it were self-evident.

As Shakespeare demonstrates in *Timon of Athens*, money is a monster that can possess or transform anything; moreover, we all know that capital, in the form of 'interest-bearing capital', is a monster capable of self-expansion. But Marx begins from the commodity, from this 'self-evident, trivial thing'. He does not do so for convenience of description. In the Hegelian system, what is immediate is merely abstract and insubstantial. But, in *Capital*, the mysteriousness of this most simple of commodities is that, while it is continuous at all levels of description, its form, as it were, changes and expands as it proceeds; the earlier terms are the key to the entirety.

---

3 Marx, First German Edition of *Capital*, in A. Dragstedt, *Value: Studies by Karl Marx* (London: New Park Publications, 1976), 34.

What distinguishes the brilliance of *Capital* as a text is not that it discloses the mystery of capitalist production, but, rather, Marx's own surprise at the 'very vexatious' characteristics of this banal and simple commodity. At a glance, the commodity is a product and a variety of use-values, but, if examined in greater depth, it is an ideational form that acts in excess of human volition precisely to restrict or constrain human beings, a form into which everything is enclosed. The established system of political economy was demolished by Marx's view of the simple and banal commodity as something 'vexatious'. And in this sense, it is precisely Marx who first discovered the commodity, and thereby the form of value.

2

It was Engels who formulated Marxism as a system, and he was literally the first reader and interpreter of Marx's texts. The problem is that he was, in a sense, an outstanding thinker with qualities entirely different from those of Marx himself. It is incorrect to suggest that Engels distorted the 'true Marx'. It is not excessive to say that, without Engels's genius, Marxism would never have enjoyed such mythical, religious power.

This is analogous to the fact it was St Paul who created Christianity. It was Paul who reinterpreted the death of Jesus, and Jesus himself can in no way be considered the creator of the Christian religion. The bulk of the force of influence that Marxism possesses does not in reality stem from Marx's texts, but, rather, exhausts his texts, stemming, instead, from a system of signification in which it appears that the texts merely express one limited aspect. No matter how much its mode of expression attempts to demarcate itself, this system of signification was born from the genealogy of Western thought, of Christianity and Platonism. Insofar as we read Marx's texts within this space, we will be unable to discover a form that fundamentally dissents from this genealogy itself.

The problem, then, is not simply to subject this or that dogma to critique. All dogma always reduces the text as 'fragment' to something transparent, a signification as 'totality'. Marx, too, begins by reading texts. His uniqueness lies not in his establishment of a philosophical system but in his attitude towards the text, and his fidelity to this attitude. *Capital* is Marx's reading of the texts of classical political economy, nothing more, nothing less. In other words, it is a mistake to seek Marx's 'thought' anywhere other than in his own mode of reading. Or, perhaps, we could say the following: Marx's 'thought' *is* precisely his method of reading itself.

We can discover this already in his 1841 doctoral thesis, *The Difference Between the Democritean and Epicurean Philosophy of Nature*. It goes without saying that, at the time, Marx was simply one amongst a number of young, left-wing Hegelians. In terms of vocabulary, in terms of the system of signification, he belonged fully to the Hegelian left. But, when we examine Marx from the standpoint of *Capital*, what is crucial is not located in his spectacular inversion of Hegel's philosophy, but in his objection to a certain specific portion of Hegel's *History of Philosophy*, the point at which Marx set out on a path no one had yet taken.

What we must pay particular attention to is the fact that Marx did not read the ancient materialist Epicurus simply as one unitary system of signification, nor did he attempt to examine simply the general differences between Epicurus and Democritus. His investigation is precisely delimited – the difference between the Democritean and Epicurean philosophy of nature.

Up to this point, in the accepted wisdom of the history of philosophy, the two thinkers' understanding of physics had been treated as largely the same, and it had been generally understood that Epicurus simply borrowed from Democritean physics, with his few minor alterations amounting to no more than arbitrary steps backward. For example, although Democritus believed that the movement of atoms was necessary and determinate, Epicurus saw in this movement contingency, swerving, and deviation. This difference between the two could be seen as prefiguring our contemporary theories of uncertainty, but prior to Marx's emphasis on this point, the difference was seen as largely meaningless. Of course, Marx did not ascribe meaning to this point as a physicist. In Marx's view, Democritus attempted to grasp the natural world by means of determinism; Epicurus, on the other hand, emphasized divergence against determination, and precisely in this sense of divergence and deviation, laid the foundations that would give rise to theories of self-consciousness, of human subjectivity and freedom.

This insight, even if we remove its genesis in the conceptual framework of the Young Hegelians, contains a decisive and crucial understanding. Rather than seeing human 'freedom' and 'subjectivity' as a priori presuppositions, such a perspective attempts rather to locate them in the 'swerves' or deviations of nature. For the Marx of the time, it was precisely his task to secure or guarantee these concepts of 'freedom' and 'subjectivity', but already here we see a perspective in which this 'freedom' and 'subjectivity' are things *forced* into existence by nature's contingent swerve. We will extend this discussion later in the present work.

What is most important for the time being is that Marx, rather than speaking of the entirety of Epicurean philosophy, considers it solely in terms of its difference with the Democritean philosophy of nature, and furthermore, speaks of a difference within what is seen as an identity.

> It is an old and entrenched prejudice to identify Democritean and Epicurean physics, so that Epicurus' modifications are seen as only arbitrary vagaries. On the other hand I am forced to

go into what seem to be microscopic examinations as far as details are concerned. But precisely because this prejudice is as old as the history of philosophy, because the differences are so concealed that they can be discovered as it were only with a microscope, it will be all the more important if, despite the interdependence of Democritean and Epicurean physics, an essential difference extending to the smallest details can be demonstrated. What can be demonstrated in the small can even more easily be shown where the relations are considered in larger dimensions, while conversely very general considerations leave doubt whether the result will hold when applied to details.[4]

What Marx emphasizes here is not merely the differences that exist between their philosophies or practices, but rather the microscopic difference between two philosophies of nature that closely resemble each other. In other words, Marx attempted to deconstruct the locus of identity itself that positioned Epicurus simply as an epigone of Democritus. The same thing can be said of *Capital*. There, Marx inherits and continues the project of numerous aspects of classical political economy, and this is precisely why non-Marxist economists treat *Capital* as itself representative of one variant of classical political economy. In a sense, they are correct.

But, of course, Marx also differs from the classical political economists, although not in the sense often propounded by Marxists themselves. This is precisely because much of what passes under the name of Marx's thought is, in fact, merely derived from classical political economy or from Hegel. For example, when Marx utilizes concepts such as 'phenomenon and essence' (Hegel) or 'labour time' (Adam Smith), he necessarily enters into the framework of their thought. If one attempts to defend Marx on these levels, Marx becomes nothing more than an epigone of Hegel or Smith. What is crucial is that Marx's uniqueness lies not in his spaces of

---

4 Marx, *The Difference between the Democritean and Epicurean Philosophy of Nature*, in MECW, vol. 1, 36.

difference with his predecessors, but, rather, lies secretly within those aspects of his thought that appear to be identical to them.

When we read Epicurus, Marx reminds us, we must overturn 'a prejudice as old as the history of philosophy'[5] – the form of identification that states Epicurus is Epicurus and Democritus is Democritus is itself as old as the history of philosophy. But this is precisely what expresses the secret of *philosophy*. Why? Because philosophy is always emerging at the very point at which it conceals the text as fragment, in other words, the text itself as signifier.

In the history of philosophy, Epicurus is a *concept*. When Marx dismantles this concept, he himself is present at the site of the becoming of the concept itself.

Nietzsche writes:

> Let us still give special consideration to the formation of concepts. Every word immediately becomes a concept, inasmuch as it is not intended to serve as a reminder of the unique and wholly individualized original experience to which it owes its birth, but must at the same time fit innumerable, more or less similar cases – which means, strictly speaking, never equal – in other words, a lot of unequal cases. Every concept originates through our equating what is unequal. No leaf ever wholly equals another, and the concept 'leaf' is formed through an arbitrary abstraction from these individual differences, through forgetting the distinctions; and now it gives rise to the idea that in nature there might be something besides the leaves which would be 'leaf' – some kind of original form after which all leaves have been woven, marked, copied, colored, curled, and painted, but by unskilled hands, so that no copy turned out to be a correct, reliable, and faithful image of the original form.[6]

---

5 Ibid.
6 Friedrich Nietzsche, 'On Truth and Lies in a Nonmoral Sense', in *Friedrich Nietzsche on Rhetoric and Language*, ed. Sander Gilman et al. (Oxford and New York: Oxford University Press, 1989), 249.

For Marx, the task is to discover not this Epicurus as 'original form', but as *difference*. If philosophical truth is located in 'metaphors worn out from frequent use' (Nietzsche), then, in an inverse sense, in order to truly think, we must think with new metaphors. At the point wherein historically accumulated 'rigour' is derided, philosophy is fundamentally shaken.

3

Thus, what we should pay particular attention to in the doctoral thesis is Marx's method of reading outlined above, along with the fact that he himself reconfirmed this reading strategy during the process of work on the *Critique of Political Economy*. For example, in the preface to the first edition of *Capital*, we can even see an identical phrasing:

> The value form, whose fully developed shape is the money form, is very elementary and simple. Nevertheless, the human mind has for more than 2,000 years sought in vain to get to the bottom of it, whilst on the other hand, to the successful analysis of much more composite and complex forms, there has been at least an approximation. Why? Because the body, as an organic whole, is more easy of study than are the cells of that body. In the analysis of economic forms, moreover, neither microscopes nor chemical reagents are of use. The force of abstraction must replace both. But in bourgeois society the commodity form of the product of labour – or the value form of the commodity – is the economic cell form. To the superficial observer, the analysis of these forms seems to turn upon minutiae. It does in fact deal with minutiae, but they are of the same order as those dealt with in microscopic anatomy.[7]

We might also put this as follows: prejudiced views of money or indeed value are as old as the history of political economy

---

7 Marx, *Capital*, vol. 1 in *MECW*, vol. 35, 8.

itself. On a broader level, classical political economy basically succeeded in elucidating the nature of economic phenomena, but in its 'minutiae', that is, in relation to the theory of the value form, was unable to achieve anything of note. The principal task of Marx's *Capital* is to overthrow the prejudices and distortions of political economy or monetary economics, predjudices as old as the discipline itself or indeed the money-economy, precisely through a microscopic explication of the value form. Yet, the microscopic detail here concerns the enigma of the money form, exactly the moment within which we can identify Marx's difference from both classical political economy and from Hegel.

Certainly, the totality of *Capital* appears to form a dialectical narrative. However, if we read this text for its minutiae, it is in the theory of the value form that Marx reveals to us the inversive nature of the dialectic – and it is not reducible to the famous imperative to 'place back on its feet' the Hegelian dialectic that is 'standing on its head'.

Obviously, Marx does not say this explicitly. On the contrary, he goes so far as to 'openly avow [himself] a pupil of that mighty thinker'. Yet, precisely at this moment, he is paradoxically free from Hegel. Marx's thought, grappling with the narrative depiction of the theory of the value form, or the 'very vexatious thing' that is the commodity, is not merely something that 'inverted the Hegelian dialectic'. Certainly, at first glance, the theory of the value form appears to simply be a means of proving the *necessity of money*. But the Hegelian-style development of the self-realization of money notwithstanding, what Marx states is that the emergence of money *conceals* or covers over the commodity or the form of value.

If there is in Marx a critique of Hegel, it exists precisely at the point in his thought where he speaks in Hegelian terms. In other words, it is in the microscopic differences, in the details, in the minor alterations, not in the 'fundamental inversion'.

I have already mentioned the question of what Marx meant by 'reading', but it is just the same for our own 'reading' of Marx. We will not take account here of the numerous places in which Marx directly criticizes Hegel. What we should read instead are the places in which he does nothing of the kind, or even those in which he speaks in certain paraphrases of Hegel.

But, in order to read in this manner, we must eliminate the disciplinary division of Marx's works that treats *Capital* as a text in political economy, *The German Ideology* as a text of philosophy, and so on. The identity of individual disciplines, stemming from their mutual differentiation, conceals the fact that they are linked together by metaphorical analogy. What allows us to strip away this concealment is the act of reading metaphorically: in other words, it is crucial to read with a view to once again restoring a certain arbitrariness to what appear to be completed, foreclosed, and fixed relations. This would mean to discover in reading, as Marx does, the text as fragment, the text that is irreducible to a transparent system of signification. Needless to say, the theory of the value form is precisely such a text. I do not think the efforts of political economists and philosophers to lend logical coherence to this theoretical work are futile; rather, I want to read in this moment towards the origin of the logical itself.

Heidegger writes:

> The greater the work of a thinker – which in no way coincides with the breadth and number of writings – the richer is what is unthought in this work, which means, that which emerges in and through this work as having not yet been thought.[8]

The richness of the theory of the value form consists in the advent of what has not yet been thought within it. Insofar as every author writes within a language and a logic, every author possesses a unique system. But the richness of a work exists

---

8 Martin Heidegger, *The Principle of Reason* [*Der Satz vom Grund*], trans. R. Lilly (Bloomington: Indiana University Press, 1996), 71.

insofar as there is a system that the author cannot control *within* the systematic structure that the author is consciously in control of, precisely in the sense that Marx expresses in his letter to Lassalle above. To read Marx is to read 'what is unthought' in the theory of the value form. In essence, I do not intend to read Marx beyond this point: the object of this study is to read Marx in the centre of his possibilities.

Chapter Two

1

Marx speaks of the enigmatic nature of the commodity, and this is where we too must begin. Everyone knows what a commodity is, but unless we cast doubt on this 'knowledge', we will be unable to see the enigma of the commodity. For example, in contrast to those orthodox Marxists who wave around copies of *Capital*, the literary critic Kobayashi Hideo once wrote:

> Marxism tells us that the commodity dominates the world. But when Marxism as a design comes to be established in one's brain, it itself has become a commodity, an imposing and elegant commodity. In turn, this transformation into a commodity has the power to force us to forget the banal fact that to humans, the world is dominated by the commodity.[1]

Evidently, the commodity in Marx has this sort of magical force. At precisely the moment one presupposes the commodity as an external object, it disappears. What is there is not the form of the commodity, but a mere thing, or indeed a human desire. It goes without saying that a mere thing is not a commodity, but is it desire that transforms a thing into a commodity? In fact, humans have desire precisely because it takes the commodity-form. Children begin to be attached to a toy that they had previously disregarded only when another

---

[1] Kobayashi Hideo, 'Samazama naru ishō' in *Kobayashi Hideo zensakuhin* (Complete Works of Kobayashi Hideo), vol. 1 (Tokyo: Shinchōsha, 2002).

child wants it. The child's desire does not transform the toy into an object of value; rather, it is precisely because the toy has value that it incites desire. Thus, whether considered from the perspective of the thing or the perspective of desire, the commodity is incapable of understanding what it is that makes a commodity.

For instance, language is neither a set of physical phonemes, nor something that simply expresses concepts. Conversely, it is precisely because we have language that these exist. So, what makes language into language? We must turn this same question towards the commodity. In classical political economy, the commodity consists of both use-value and exchange-value. But use-value and exchange-value only come into existence insofar as something takes the commodity-form. It is the same phenomenon as in the case of language, in which a word is the articulation between phoneme and concept. In as much as the analysis ends there, however, we will remain unable to glimpse the secret of the commodity or of language. To put it another way, the secret of the commodity-form lies precisely in its 'power to force us to forget' the secret of the commodity itself. Nevertheless, let us begin from the analysis of the commodity-form. Marx writes as follows:

> Commodities come into the world in the shape of use-values, articles, or goods, such as iron, linen, corn, &c. This is their plain, homely, natural form (*Naturalform*). They are, however, commodities, only because they are something two-fold, both objects of utility, and, at the same time, depositories of value. They manifest themselves therefore as commodities, or have the form of commodities, only in so far as they have two forms, a physical or natural form, and a value-form. The reality of the value of commodities differs in this respect from Dame Quickly, that we don't know 'where to have it'. The value of commodities is the very opposite of the coarse materiality of their substance, not an atom of matter enters into its composition.

Turn and examine a single commodity, by itself, as we will, yet in so far as it remains an object of value, it seems impossible to grasp it. If, however we bear in mind that the value of commodities has a purely social reality, and that they acquire this reality only in so far as they are expressions or embodiments of one identical social substance, viz., human labour, it follows as a matter of course, that value can only manifest itself in the social relation of commodity to commodity.[2]

What Marx refers to as commodity fetishism is nothing more than the situation in which the 'natural form', that is, the physical object, carries with it the 'value form'. But this is equally applicable to all signs. Thus, Marx is always speaking by means of analogies to the situation of language: 'To stamp an object of utility as a value, is just as much a social product as language.'[3] We can go back as far as *The German Ideology* in following Marx on this point:

> Man also possesses 'consciousness', but, even so, not inherent, not 'pure' consciousness. From the start the 'spirit' is afflicted with the curse of being 'burdened' with matter, which here makes its appearance in the form of agitated layers of air, sounds, in short, of language. Language is as old as consciousness, language is practical consciousness that exists also for other men, and for that reason alone it really exists for me personally as well; language, like consciousness, only arises from the need, the necessity, of intercourse [*Verkehr*] with other men.[4]

Marx refuses any concept of 'pure consciousness', that is, any concept of transcendental meaning. It is always and from the outset 'burdened with matter' and can never be separated from the 'agitated layers of air' that make up its 'natural

---

2 Marx, *MEW*, Bd. 23, 61–2. Translation modified.
3 Marx, *Capital*, vol. 1 in *MECW*, vol.35, 85.
4 Marx, *The German Ideology*, in *MECW*, vol. 5, 44.

form'. Marx does not subject metaphysical idealism to critique simply by positing matter against it, since the 'agitated layers' of air are not in and of themselves language. So, what makes language language? It is the same enquiry that makes the commodity a commodity: and it is precisely at this point that the 'value-form' comes into question.

2

Saussure attempted to clarify the object of linguistics as the analysis of the conditions that make language into language, excluding from it these 'agitated layers of air' as the object not of linguistics, but of phonology. Likewise, Marx excluded from his thought the consideration of the concrete, physical commodity, leaving it the object of a mere 'commoditology' (*shōhingaku*). As a result, Saussure locates the essence of language in the articulation between the *signifier* (phoneme) and the *signified* (concept). However, this was not a particularly new insight. What was new in Saussure is that he attempted to see language as value. In other words, he treats language as a system of the differential relations of signifiers, in which meaning is not present a priori but located within a system of the ascription of difference, that is, it emerges from the interval between words or terms. This is a perspective that can only develop insofar as one dissociates the analysis from the single unit of the word. Metaphysics sees meaning as transcendental, but only because it enacts an active forgetting of the fact that meaning is only ever located within a system of differential relations.

Marx states that the classical political economists, in differentiating use-value from exchange-value, conceived of the commodity in isolation. But these differentiations emerge from the fact that the commodity is the value-form, a differential relation. Marx corrects himself on this point as follows:

When, at the beginning of this chapter, we said, in common parlance, that a commodity is both a use-value and an exchange-value, we were, accurately speaking, wrong. A commodity is a use-value or object of utility, and a value. It manifests itself as this two-fold thing, that it is, as soon as its value assumes an independent form – viz., the form of exchange-value. It never assumes this form when isolated, but only when placed in a value or exchange relation with another commodity of a different kind. When once we know this, such a mode of expression does no harm; it simply serves as an abbreviation.[5]

However, it should be said that this expression is, in fact, always quite harmful. Precisely at the moment when we reject the notion that the single commodity has an intrinsic value, we discover the value-form, but the above 'common parlance' will always land us back at the starting point.

Marx writes: 'It is one of the chief failings of classical economy that it has never succeeded, by means of its analysis of commodities, and, in particular, of their value, in discovering that form under which value becomes exchange-value. Even Adam Smith and Ricardo, the best representatives of the school, treat the form of value as a thing of no importance, as having no connexion with the inherent nature of commodities.'[6] However, this is precisely because Smith and Ricardo treated money as a simple presupposition. Money provides an illusory appearance, as if, within each commodity, there existed a value that could be expressed in a certain magnitude of money. That is, the money-form conceals the fact that value is located within the value-form, or the relation between differing use-values.

As is well known, at the outset of *Capital*, Marx argues that in order for two different commodities to be equal in value, there must necessarily be a 'common something' that they

---

5 Marx, *Capital*, 71.
6 Ibid., 91 n. 2.

share, and this is nothing other than human labour objectified in the commodity. However, this is simply money expressed in different terms, and, in that sense, does not go beyond the classical political economists as an observation. He instead reduces the 'identity' of different commodities to explain the secret of their equivalence. But this identity is realized by means of money. It is precisely the money-form that conceals the value-form. Thus, when he enquires into the origins of the money-form, Marx discards these notions of 'equivalence' and 'commonality', because they appear within the concealment of the value-form.

First, Marx explicates the 'elementary or accidental form of value' as follows:

> x commodity A = y commodity B, *or*
> x commodity A is worth y commodity B.
> 20 yards of linen = 1 coat, or
> 20 Yards of linen are worth 1 coat.[7]

In the above example, when the 'linen expresses its value in the coat', Marx states that the linen is in the relative form of value, while the coat is in the equivalent form. In other words, what Marx argues here is not that the linen is equivalent to the coat, but, rather, that the value of the linen is expressed by the use-value of the coat: 'The value of the commodity linen is expressed by the bodily form of the commodity coat, the value of one by the use-value of the other.'[8] However, this is not because the value of linen exists as something inherent or transcendental. Rather, simply because the linen and the coat have two differing use-values, 'value' appears from the relation between them.

This relation itself is the value-form, that is, the articulation of the relative form of value and the equivalent form of value: 'The relative form and the equivalent form are two

---

7 Ibid., 58.
8 Ibid., 62.

intimately connected, mutually dependent and inseparable elements of the expression of value; but, at the same time, are mutually exclusive, antagonistic extremes – i.e., poles of the same expression'.[9] If we align this insight with Saussure, the relative form of value plays the role of the signified, while the equivalent form plays the role of the signifier, and the value-form, as their articulation, constitutes the sign. Considered in terms of Marx's example, the coat as use-value is the signifier.

3

Marx then takes up what he calls the 'expanded form of value':

$$z \text{ Com. A} = u \text{ Com. B } or$$
$$= v \text{ Com. C } or$$
$$= w \text{ Com. D } or$$
$$= \text{ Com. E } or$$
$$= \&c.$$

This is a chain of the relative relationships of all differing commodities to each, a chain without a centre. It is what we might call a 'system of relation without a centre'. Marx describes this apparent 'defect' as follows:

> In the first place, the relative expression of value is incomplete because the series representing it is interminable. The chain of which each equation of value is a link, is liable at any moment to be lengthened by each new kind of commodity that comes into existence and furnishes the material for a fresh expression of value.[10]

Thus, Marx explicates the necessity of the appearance of one commodity that could act as the centre of this chain, that is, the general form of value or the money-form. But it must be

---

9 Ibid., 58.
10 Ibid., 74.

said that this depiction remains inverted. This is because it is precisely the 'total or expanded form of value' that is this 'system of relation without a centre', finally discovered when it decentres the general form of value or money-form. Within linguistics, Saussure arrived at this same point, just as Lévi-Strauss did within anthropology.

To say that this form is incomplete obviously stems from a teleological conception that sees the money-form as a complete entity. Far from being incomplete, it is the primordial scene that we lose sight of within what is 'completed'. Conversely to Marx's dialectical-teleological depiction, we must persist with this vision he detected. This is because this vision is the sole means to suggest that something transcendental like essence or concept could only ever be inverted. It appears that Marx writes that the development from the 'elementary form of value' to the 'money-form' is a logical necessity:

> We perceive, at first sight, the deficiencies of the elementary form of value: it is a mere germ, which must undergo a series of metamorphoses before it can ripen into the price-form.
>
> The expression of the value of commodity A in terms of any other commodity B, merely distinguishes the value from the use-value of A, and therefore places A merely in a relation of exchange with a single different commodity, B; but it is still far from expressing A's *qualitative identity, and quantitative proportionality*, to all commodities.[11]

But this elementary form of value is not merely something 'deficient' that must ripen into a more complete form. All commodities are given existence by means of the 'qualitative identity and quantitative proportionality' of the money-form, the commodity that furnishes a centre through which all other commodities can be placed into relation. But this is not simply present from the beginning. Consequently, the

---

11 Ibid., 72.

'common something' that must be present is merely the *latent* money-form. The elementary form of value is often conflated with barter, and the expansion of the barter system is frequently seen as giving rise to the general form of value, or the money-form. In fact, in Part 2, 'The Exchange Process', Marx himself suggests as much. It ought to go without saying, but if one takes this perspective, the meaning and importance of value-form theory completely vanishes. The elementary form of value is disclosed insofar as it decentres money (the general equivalent), which conceals the value-form itself.

In the case of the 'total or expanded form of value', the relative form of value (the signified) and the equivalent form of value (the signifier) never take on a fixed relation. For instance, when we point out that the value of the linen is expressed by the use-value of the coat, it does not matter at all if we switch the positions of the linen and the coat. In other words, there is no such thing as 'value' but the *differential* relation of use-values – or, more accurately, the play of *difference* itself – that is at the foundation. On this point, we can go back against Marx's own order of description and deal with the problems contained in the 'elementary and accidental form of value'.

Certainly, we cannot accomplish our task simply by decentring the money-form. The problem is to clarify *why* and *how* this centring took place at all. In other words, when one commodity is centralized, it erases the relational play of the signifier, constructing an identity, and attributing to it a transcendental value; nevertheless, we cannot allow ourselves to be satisfied, like the structuralists, by simply pointing instead to this 'system of relation without a centre'.

Rather, what we should cast doubt on is the thought of 'systems' and 'structures'. For instance, even if money is decentred as a single commodity, the centre remains within the system itself. That is, something systemic that makes it into a system remains in a latent sense. In the case of *langue* as a system, there is no centre like money, but the Platonic common sense that finds an inherent meaning (concept) in each language itself upholds a sort of unseen centre, and it is precisely for this reason that Saussure puts forward a rejection to it, in the form of the system of relation without centre. But Saussure never considered how it is that such a system emerges at all. On this point, the structuralists assumed that it was the null or zero symbol that made a system a system. But this is precisely something transcendental – the structuralists did no more than reject the transcendental at the level of appearance.

In this sense, structuralism is foreclosed into the binary of signifier and signified, or in another sense, culture and nature; it remains in the domain of metaphysics. Insofar as Marx thought within the binary of use-value and value, he remains trapped within the *metaphysics of money*. As we saw earlier, at the foundation is this voluntary relation between one use-value (signifier) and another use-value or signifier. The value-form is a figurative or embodying language, so to speak. In the case of phonetic language, this is already concealed.

For instance, against the perspective that sees two qualitatively different commodities as equal on the basis of the equal labour they include, Marx writes:

> Hence, when we bring the products of our labour into relation with each other as values, it is not because we see in these articles the material receptacles of homogeneous human labour. *Quite the contrary*: whenever, by an exchange, we equate as values our different products, by that very act, we also equate, as human labour, the different kinds of labour expended upon them. *We are not aware of this, nevertheless we do it*. Value, therefore, does not stalk about with a label describing what it is. It is value, rather, that converts every product into a social hieroglyphic. *Later on*, we try to decipher the hieroglyphic, to get behind the secret of our own social products; for to stamp an object of utility as a value, is just as much a social product as *language*. The recent scientific discovery, that the products

of labour, so far as they are values, are but material expressions of the human labour spent in their production, marks, indeed, an epoch in the history of the development of the human race, but, by no means, dissipates the mist through which the social character of labour appears to us to be an objective character of the products themselves.[12]

When he says that 'we are not aware of this, nevertheless we do it', Marx is speaking of the unconscious in downright Freudian terms. Lacan emphasized that the unconscious is structured like a language. In the same way, the value-form, under erasure within the form of money, is precisely what Marx referred to here as a 'hieroglyph'. It is invisible within our consciousness; only its results are reflected. As Freud argued, to be conscious of something is to phonetically lingualize it. What we consciously cognize merely takes the form of money as phonetic script. Political economy begins from this 'consciousness'. In other words, to say this is also to emphasize that political economy has always tacitly presupposed money. Insofar as every reflection or analysis, no matter how rigorous, is located within this always-already formalized 'consciousness', its results are always mistaken for its causes.

For example, when a neurotic is afraid of heights, we often say that he or she is afraid *because* of heights. But heights in and of themselves are not the 'cause' of the neurotic's fear. In the same way, we equate two different products not *because* of the common objectified human labour within them; rather, it is merely the result of an entire series of things that are already concealed with regard to this 'consciousness'.

Thus, we cannot understand why Marx argues that his is the first attempt at a theory of the value-form in the history of humanity without seeing it in this context. Indeed, it appears to be explicated dialectically, as if the 'contradiction' between

---

12 Ibid., 85.

use-value and exchange-value is sublated in the money-form. However, 'contradiction', and indeed the 'dialectic' itself, are here merely rationalized in the aftermath of the becoming they have already attained. Philosophy is nothing more than a type of neurotic rationalization, foreclosed into 'consciousness' as result of the nexus of money and phonetic script.

The concept of the unconscious is generally associated with Freud, but as is clear from *The Interpretation of Dreams* or *Studies on Hysteria*, Freud's interest lay in the fact that the 'unconscious' existed as something linguistic. 'This seems at first to be a striking example of the genesis of hysterical symptoms through symbolization by means of verbal expression.'[13] If we follow Lacan's critique, that psychoanalysis completely lost sight of this point, we can equally say that the same is true of Marx's theory of the value-form. Here Marx, for the first time, puts forward the hieroglyphic mode typically concealed in the money-form/pre-conscious, but later Marxisms simply reduced this question to something *philosophical*; Marx here is precisely attempting to radically critique 'philosophy', including the dialectic itself.

4

When we consider value, we are forced to confront the following question: what is the basis that allows two qualitatively different things to be equal in value? This is not merely a question for political economy, but one that encompasses all problems posed by the concept of value in general.

'Have these genealogists of morality up to now ever remotely dreamt that, for example, the main moral concept '*Schuld*' ('guilt') descends from the very material concept of

---

13 Sigmund Freud, *Studies on Hysteria*, trans. James Strachey (New York: Basic Books, 2000), 179.

'*Schulden*' ('debts')?"[14] asks Nietzsche. He argues that the moralist, whether thinking the forms of the passions fragmentarily or systematically, exists within the discovery of the *relation* of credit and debt. What I hate about that man, Dostoevsky's famous protagonist states, is that he is kind to me despite the fact that I treated him horribly. This is exactly like the person who borrows money and does not pay it back, but nevertheless despises the lender. In other words, in Nietzsche's thought, the consciousness of sin is the sentiment of debt, and hatred manifests in its denial.

However, what is crucial is that Nietzsche discovered the inversion that makes equivalent completely heterogeneous things at the base of this relation of credit and debt. For instance, the conception of equality among human beings essentially means the equivalence of qualitatively different people. We take this as something rather self-evident, or we reject it in the name of 'nature'. But the advantage of Nietzsche's thought is that its point of departure is the fundamental question of what equivalence actually is, rather than to simply take a position in favour of either equality or inequality. In comparison with Nietzsche, thinkers like Rousseau or Sade merely place nature and society into an abstract opposition, eliding the more essential question.

> Throughout most of human history, punishment has *not* been meted out *because* the miscreant was held responsible for his act, therefore it was *not* assumed that the guilty party alone should be punished: – but rather, as parents still punish their children, it was out of anger over some wrong that had been suffered, directed at the perpetrator, – but this anger was held in check and modified by the idea that every injury has its *equivalent* which can be paid in compensation, if only through the *pain* of the person who injures. And where did

---

14 Friedrich Nietzsche, *On the Genealogy of Morality*, ed. Keith Ansell Pearson (Cambridge: Cambridge University Press, 2006), 39.

this primeval, deeply-rooted and perhaps now ineradicable idea gain its power, this idea of an equivalence between injury and pain? I have already let it out: in the contractual relationship between *creditor* and *debtor*, which is as old as the very conception of a 'legal subject' and itself refers back to the basic forms of buying, selling, bartering, trade and traffic.[15]

A parent who beats a child does so out of a violent sense of anger, but the parent will perhaps imagine that they do so out of a desire to discipline or educate. Similarly, although punishment emerges from anger directed against harm caused, it is also seen as an educational or corrective measure taken vis-à-vis the offender. This way of thinking is classically summarized by Hegel's perspective in *The Philosophy of Right*: because the offender in essence violates themselves by committing the offence, punishment is merely a means of self-recovery or rehabilitation. At the foundation of this mode of thought there lies the notion that crime and punishment, or damage and suffering, are, in essence, equivalent.

To what can we attribute this notion, that within all damage or harm caused there is something equivalent, 'this primeval, deeply-rooted and perhaps now ineradicable idea'? Nietzsche discovers it within the form of buying and selling, 'trade and traffic'. With this transposition, let us note that the problem becomes trickier. Nietzsche's transposition of the problem into 'buying and selling' should not be confused with a mere transfer of the problem into the field of political economy. Conversely, it fundamentally calls economics itself (which presupposes money) into question. When Marx, at the outset of *Capital*, asks what in fact is the 'equivalent form' of different commodities, he condenses into this question every possible problem of the conundrum.

---

15 Ibid., 40.

Nietzsche once wrote that 'every concept arises from the making-equivalent of unequal things.'[16] To put it another way, it begins in metaphor, but first arises only when the metaphor ceases to be metaphorical. Thus, we cannot be misled by the division between economic concepts and ethical concepts; what is in question is the metaphysics that subtends every field of inquiry.

5

On Aristotle's understanding of value, Marx writes as follows:

> In the first place, [Aristotle] clearly enunciates that the money-form of commodities is only the further development of the simple form of value – *i.e.*, of the expression of the value of one commodity in some other commodity taken at random; for he says:
>
> 5 beds = 1 house
> is not to be distinguished from
> 5 beds = so much money.
>
> He further sees that the value-relation which gives rise to this expression makes it necessary that the house should qualitatively be made the equal of the bed, and that, without such an equalisation, these two clearly different things could not be compared with each other as commensurable quantities. 'Exchange', he says, 'cannot take place without equality, and equality not without commensurability'. Here, however, he comes to a stop, and gives up the further analysis of the form of value. 'It is, however, in reality, impossible, that such unlike things can be commensurable' – *i.e.*, qualitatively equal. Such an equalisation can only be something foreign to their real nature, consequently only 'a makeshift for practical purposes'.

---

16 Nietzsche, 'On Truth and Lies in a Nonmoral Sense', 249. Translation modified.

Aristotle therefore, himself, tells us, what barred the way to his further analysis; it was the absence of any concept of value. What is that equal something, that common substance, which admits of the value of the beds being expressed by a house? Such a thing, in truth, cannot exist, says Aristotle. And why not? Compared with the beds, the house does represent something equal to them, in so far as it represents what is really equal, both in the beds and the house. And that is – human labour.

There was, however, an important fact which prevented Aristotle from seeing that, to attribute value to commodities, is merely a mode of expressing all labour as equal human labour, and consequently as labour of equal quality. Greek society was founded upon slavery, and had, therefore, for its natural basis, the inequality of men and of their labour-powers. The secret of the expression of value, namely, that all kinds of labour are equal and equivalent, because, and so far as they are human labour in general, cannot be deciphered, until the notion of human equality has already acquired the fixity of a popular prejudice. This, however, is possible only in a society in which the great mass of the produce of labour takes the form of commodities, in which, consequently, the dominant relation between man and man, is that of owners of commodities. The brilliancy of Aristotle's genius is shown by this alone, that he discovered, in the expression of the value of commodities, a relation of equality. The peculiar conditions of the society in which he lived, alone prevented him from discovering what, 'in truth', was at the bottom of this equality.[17]

At first glance, it appears that Marx is merely pointing out the historical limits within which Aristotle wrote. For instance, for Aristotle, the making-equivalent of different things is merely 'a makeshift for practical purposes', without a common substance that we ought to seek. In contrast, the thinkers

---

17 Marx, *Capital*, 69–70.

of national economy (Smith and Ricardo) discovered this 'common substance' as the human labour included within it. What made Aristotle unable to see this was the fact that his own society was based on slave labour, rather than on any sort of equality of labour. On the surface, this is Marx's point.

However, if this is the case, why does Marx develop a critique of the classical political economists in the following manner?

> Hence, when we bring the products of our labour into relation with each other as values, it is not because we see in these articles the material receptacles of homogeneous human labour. ... The recent scientific discovery, that the products of labour, so far as they are values, are but material expressions of the human labour spent in their production, marks, indeed, an epoch in the history of the development of the human race, but, by no means, dissipates the mist through which the social character of labour appears to us to be an objective character of the products themselves.[18]

In other words, to see the identity of value in the identity of the human being or in his or her labour power is tautological, and provides no resolution of the problem. Although it asks why qualitatively different things should be identical, it merely answers by saying that they are. Nevertheless, here a certain thought of 'human equality' has been silently incorporated into the question. As we stated at the outset, this entire problem has its foundations in the question of human equality, so the crucial question of why and how qualitatively different things take on an equivalent form is merely bypassed, resulting in tautology. What we today call 'world religion' emerged against the backdrop of the ancient city, or to put it in other terms, what we might call 'ancient capitalism'. Human equality is the product of a money economy, but

---

18 Ibid., 84–5.

the secret of money was not called into question. Rather, what is called into question are the foundations of this singularity called money, or God.

Socialism, for instance, takes as its point of departure a thinking of the identical nature of human beings. It goes without saying that Marx undertook a total critique of this type of socialist idealism, but this is precisely because he uniquely possessed the specific insight into the question of *value*. Classical political economy saw a qualitatively homogeneous human labour as the source of how two qualitatively different use-values could be equivalent. This is, in fact, a conception that presupposes the existence of the money-form, treating money as immanent within each individual commodity. In other words, although in such a perspective it appears that each commodity first comes to possess a 'shared substance' through the formation of money, in fact the belief was simply that each commodity did indeed possess this shared substance.

This is exactly parallel to God in Christianity, who relates to every human individually, thus providing a structural proof of their equality. Marx criticizes Proudhon's conception of a socialism in which money would be eliminated, but commodities would remain.[19] In a sense, we can place this alongside Nietzsche's critique of a socialism in which God is eliminated, but the thought of equality remains. To negate money, to negate God, still means nothing at this stage, since from the earlier viewpoints, money is immanent in each commodity, just as God is immanent in each person. Once again, although they might try to be aware of it, nevertheless they are still doing it.

Marx writes: 'The secret of the expression of value, namely, that all kinds of labour are equal and equivalent, because, and so far as they are human labour in general, cannot be deciphered, until the notion of human equality has already

---

19 See Marx, *The Poverty of Philosophy*, in MECW, vol. 6.

acquired the fixity of a popular prejudice.'[20] But Marx, of course, does not take 'human equality' to be a sort of a priori truth, rather it is a concept that itself becomes possible 'only in a society in which the great mass of the produce of labour takes the form of commodities, in which, consequently, the dominant relation between man and man, is that of owners of commodities.'[21] In other words, homogeneous human labour is not something that is simply given from the outset, but, instead, something that appears precisely through the expansion of the monetary economy.

Because the money economy existed only as an exterior portion of the society in which he lived, Aristotle could be sceptical as to the identity of qualitatively different things. He thought that in each single commodity, there existed no such thing as an immanent essential value. Yet he never doubted that behind each word lay a transcendental concept (Idea). Metaphysics insists on meaning as transcendental idea, despite the fact that words exist only within differential relations. In this sense, the money-form, and the modes of thought based on its presupposition, are metaphysical, and its critique is not confined to the sphere of economy, but becomes a more general critique of all metaphysics. Or perhaps it is more appropriate to say that the money-form exists precisely at the foundation of metaphysics. It is for this reason that the question of the origins of the money-form is so difficult, because the question itself is always falling into the metaphysical trap. And the dialectical mode of presentation in Marx is no exception.

---

20 Marx, *Capital*, 70.
21 Ibid.

Chapter Three

1

Up until this point, we have investigated the various questions that surround the money-form, but we must now ask *why* these questions play such an important role for the totality of *Capital*. Of course, we cannot simply speak of the entirety of *Capital*. But Marxian economists often treat the theory of the value-form as a portion of the text that merely gives proof for the necessity of money. Yet the theory of the value-form itself is precisely what clarifies the secret of capital, a theoretical analysis capable of elucidating the foundations of capital as a whole, even without the supposition of 'labour time'.

The idea that the value of a commodity is based on the labour contained within it has existed since the work of William Petty. In Adam Smith, this concept is grasped quantitatively as 'labour time', but such a concept only becomes possible with the establishment of mechanical production, in which the individual and qualitative differences of labour are erased. But, in Smith, this 'epochal discovery' still does not lead him to be able to clarify how such labour time applies to products produced by means of non-mechanical production. To put it another way, Smith was never able to make clear why it is that the capitalist system, based on mechanical production, spreads across the landscape of all production, including non-commodity production, becoming capable of organizing the entirety of this space within capitalist society.

Every product passes through the money-form, and is thereby attributed the same external appearance as those produced mechanically. Although mechanical production is merely one aspect of the totality of production, it is what gives all production the external appearance of the form of the capitalist system. Thus, in order to explicate the nature of capitalist society, we must inquire into the origins of the money-form, which is the condition of possibility for this aspect, and even if Marx adopted the theory of labour-time from classical political economy, he problematized the riddle that precedes it theoretically:

> Circulation bursts through all restrictions as to time, place, and individuals, imposed by direct barter, and this it effects by splitting up, into the antithesis of a sale and a purchase, the direct identity that in barter does exist between the alienation of one's own and the acquisition of some other man's product.[1]

What Marx means here in terms of money is precisely the letter, or script. For example, in spoken language, there must be a listener. If the other party in conversation says the word 'dog', we can ascertain what type of dog they mean. But, if the word 'dog' is written, we do not know what type of dog is intended. Unlike conversation, script can be read anywhere and at any time. The 'direct identity' of speaking and listening is 'split up' by the letter or script.

But, if we were to problematize Marx's way of writing, it appears as if direct exchange existed at the very beginning, which is then followed by a sort of mediated exchange. Perhaps this is indeed the proper sequence. First we speak, then we learn to write. However, what we should be wary of here is that this ordering parallels exactly the notion that there is from the outset an 'interiority' that later comes to be 'exteriorized'.

Why do we 'write' at all? Because we possess something that in the end cannot be fully satisfied solely by speaking.

---

[1] Marx, *Capital*, vol. 1 in *MECW*, vol. 35, 123.

This is precisely what people call 'interiority'. A child who is not yet literate does not have this sort of interiority; it is the result of script or letters. Nevertheless, people equally conceive of script as if it were the thing most estranged from interiority. The reason for this is that script is generally phonetic script, and is thus frequently seen to be simply the expression of phonemes. Thus, we must try to conceive of money/phonetic script not from the standpoint of interiority or the value that inheres in the commodity, but from the standpoint of what Marx understood as the value-form as hieroglyphic. It is not that script was invented to express some transcendental meaning or value; on the contrary, it was precisely script that brought about these things. This fact itself is concealed within the form of consciousness that is the result of the establishment of money/phonetic script.

In general, conceptions of money are metaphysical insofar as they are transfixed by the concept of money merely as the measure of value. Certainly, Saussure was no exception to this. However, what allowed him to take language as the value-form – in other words, as a relation of difference of the signifier – is precisely that he was able to avoid all such conventional wisdom in relation to the concept of language itself. But when it comes to thinking the similarity of money to language, what dominates Saussure's understanding is the 'old and entrenched prejudice' haunting the history of Western thought.

For instance, Saussure eliminates the analysis of any other script systems (such as Chinese characters), limiting his discussion to alphabets or phonographic script. However, this is because he sees script as something that expresses phonemes, rendering it secondary, a conception already prevalent since Plato. This is just the same as the conception of money as the manifestation of the value of the commodity or its measure. Classical political economy treated money as secondary by means of the labour theory of value. Thus, money becomes something superfluous, and it is from here that the conception of money as the 'root of all evil' is derived.

In fact, Proudhon, basing himself on classical political economy, advocated the elimination of money and proposed a theory of 'labour money'. Generally speaking, those ideologues who abhor money have some sort of 'direct exchange' in mind. Just as Plato and Rousseau abhorred script, they think as if there were the possibility of a sort of internal, direct exchange as communication. However, what is 'direct' or 'internal' is itself a product of money/phonetic script, and in the perversion of this perspectival approach is precisely a metaphysics.

In this schema of money-form = phonetic script = consciousness, the value-form is always-already concealed. But why is this important at all? Because, despite the fact that this characteristic of money is the foundation of the 'transformation of money into capital', this aspect of it is simultaneously hidden. If money were merely something that expressed the value of a commodity, the M (money) –C (commodity) –M' (M+ΔM) process would be impossible.[2] In other words, without the possessor of money, who purchases a commodity, and through selling it gains ΔM (surplus value), the emergence of capital itself would be impossible.

However, where there is money, there is bound to be merchant capital. This is not because humans characteristically seek profits or anything of the kind. Precisely only at the point when the necessary foundations through which exchange generates profits (surplus value) are in place can any such sort of 'human nature' emerge at all. For the time being, whether we examine the process from M–C or C–M', there is no scope for the generation of surplus, except by fraud. But temporary fraud is incapable of producing the continuous foundations

---

2 [Trans.] In most Japanese-language Marxist theory, the original German abbreviations in Marx's formulas – W (*Ware*) for commodity, G (*Geld*) for money – are retained, but these have here been switched to the standard English terms.

of capital – self-expanding money. The key is that in fact such foundations can *only* emerge insofar as M–C and C–M' are uncoupled or delinked in terms of both time and place. In other words, money is not a simple value-measure that expresses value, but is rather nothing more than what we might call *an opaque text*. Marx sees the general possibility of crisis in this type of separation, but the conditions of possibility of crisis and the conditions of possibility of capital itself are located at the same point.

2

To put it simply, merchant capital arises from buying something cheaply in one region and selling it for more in another region. However, the merchant is not a swindler, nor is the merchant practising a form of unequal exchange. The value of one commodity is not immanent, but exists simply through its value-relation with all other commodities. But, once it takes the money-form, it comes to be expressed quantitatively. The same commodity is cheap in one place and expensive in another simply because the *relations* between different commodities are themselves different from place to place. When these relations are erased by the money-form, it appears exactly as if there were an independent, immanent value. Thus, the differential as system of relation appears as quantitative difference by means of money.

That the same commodity is cheap in one place and expensive in another rests on the fact that value is not immanent in it, but merely present in a system of differential relations. Then, when it is transformed quantitatively by means of money, this difference as system appears as the price differential of a single commodity. Merchant capital depends on this price differential. In order for this to be the case, these two systems of value must be mutually isolated.

Consequently, merchant capital can only exist in the interval between mutually distant, differing systems. 'The trading peoples of antiquity, like the gods of Epicurus, are located in the *intermundia*, in the spaces between the worlds, or rather like the Jews in the pores of Polish society.'[3] Of course, this is by no means exclusive to the 'trading peoples'. For instance, Sakamoto Ryoma recognized price differentials between Nagasaki, Shimonoseki and Osaka, and organized commercial shipping to exploit this gap. But what rendered this possible was that those regions were fully separate and possessed different value systems.

Paul Valéry writes as follows:

> After all, a work of art is an object, a human product, made with a view to affecting certain individuals in a certain way. Works of art are either objects in the material sense of the term, or sequences of acts, as in the case of drama or the dance, or else summations of successive impressions that are also produced by acts, as in music. We may attempt to define our notion of art by an analysis based on these objects, which may be taken as the only positive elements in our investigations: considering these objects and progressing on the one hand to their authors and on the other hand to those whom they affect, we find that the phenomenon of art can be represented by two quite distinct transformations. (We have here the same relation as that which prevails in economics between production and consumption.)
>
> What is extremely important is to note that these two transformations – the author's modification of the manufactured object and the change which the object or work brings about in the consumer – are quite independent. It follows that we should always consider them separately.

---

3 Marx, *Economic Manuscripts of 1857–58* [*Grundrisse*], in MECW, vol. 29, 233.

CHAPTER THREE

Any proposition involving all three terms, an author, a work, a spectator or listener, is meaningless – for you will never find all three terms united in observation. ...

I shall go further – and here I come to a point you will no doubt find strange and paradoxical, if you have not come to that conclusion about what I have already said: art as a *value* (for basically, we are studying the problem of value) depends essentially on this non-identification, this need for an intermediary between producer and consumer. It is essential that there should be something irreducible between them, that there should be no direct communication, and that the work, the medium, should not give the person it affects anything that can be reduced to an idea of the author's person and thinking. ...

There will never be any accurate way of comparing what has happened in the two minds of author/artist and other or reader; and moreover, if what has happened in the one were communicated directly to the other, all art would collapse, all the effects of art would disappear. The whole effect of art, the effort that the author's work demands of the consumer, would be impossible without the interposition, between the author and his audience, of a new and impenetrable element capable of acting upon other men's being.[4]

Thus, Valéry seeks the ultimate foundation of the value of the work in the fact that the two transformations are mutually severed from each other and opaque. What he directly criticizes is the Hegelian conception of aesthetics. That is, Hegel's aesthetics – like the aesthetic theories of Marxism – locates itself in a position from which it can observe these two transformations at the same time, turning history into something transparent.

What Valéry here calls 'value' corresponds to what Marx conceives of as surplus value. Just as Valéry's reflections

---

4 Paul Valéry, 'Reflections on Art', in *Paul Valéry, Aesthetics*, trans. Ralph Manheim (New York: Pantheon, 1964), 142–3, translation modified; 'Réflexions sur l'art', in Œuvres complètes *de Paul Valéry* (Paris: Gallimard, 1957).

41

concern the *written* work or text, when we think of surplus value, we must remain aware of the correspondence between money and (phonetic) script. For example, Saussure thought language in its similarities to money, but, just as he erased the problem of script from his theory of language, he was only able to theorize money as a simple measure of value. In other words, any attempt to relegate the equation of money–script to a secondary phenomenon, whether in economics or in linguistics, will inevitably be led into a shared error.

When we have the process of commodity C–money M–commodity C′, Saussure would see this as message–code–message, taking 'code' to signify 'language' (*langue*). Talcott Parsons, who attempted to apply linguistics to the economic sphere, conceived of money as a form of code. But he began from the point that Saussure had not fundamentally understood what money was. If, for example, the circulation process C–M–C′ was what Saussure thought, then it is not possible that it should also be its inverse or verso, the process M–C–M′ (M+ΔM). A linguist would postulate here the 'ideal speaker-hearer'. However, it is not that this idealized, clear communication becomes unclear due to the mediation of script; rather, in precisely the inverse sense, it is that clear communication (exchange) itself is nothing more than a metaphysical abstraction born from phonetic script or money. Roman Jakobson optimistically spoke of installing linguistics as the foundation of its proximate sciences, but in reality what must be called into question is the origin of linguistics itself.

3

In contrast to the merchant who gains profit from the circulation process, the religious leader or philosopher would typically have seen in such a process an example of unequal exchange, or moral injustice. But the conception of 'equal exchange' is itself a metaphysics that posits in thought an inherent value to the commodity, corresponding to the disdain the philosophers had for the mediational or secondary category of writing or script.

Marx gives little consideration to merchant capital, the most ancient form of capital's existence, the form of capital born from the M–C–M' process of circulation. When he speaks of the 'transformation of money into capital', Marx dismisses the consideration of merchant capital because, for him, what was crucial was to speak of the 'secrets' of industrial capital, and, in order to do so, it was necessary to negate the illusion posited by merchant capital, the illusion that it is the circulation process that gives rise to surplus value. On this point, he was influenced by the attitude of classical political economy, which emerged in opposition to the theorists of mercantilism:

> It is true, commodities may be sold at prices deviating from their values, but these deviations are to be considered as infractions of the laws of the exchange of commodities, which in its normal state is an exchange of equivalents, consequently, no method for increasing value. ...
>
> The creation of surplus-value, and therefore the conversion of money into capital, can consequently be explained neither on the assumption that commodities are sold above their value, nor that they are bought below their value. ...
>
> The capitalist class, as a whole, in any country, cannot overreach themselves. Turn and twist then as we may, the fact remains unaltered. If equivalents are exchanged, no surplus-value results, and if non-equivalents are exchanged, still no surplus-value. Circulation, or the exchange of commodities, begets no value.[5]

In the broad sense, there should be nothing beyond commodity exchange able to give rise to surplus value. The production process, too, must be thought within the question of 'exchange'

---

5 Marx, *Capital*, 169; 172; 173–4.

between the possessors of commodities. It appears that Marx is saying that industrial capital gains surplus value not from the circulation process, but from the production process. However, the production process itself has no relation to value, and value, indeed surplus value too, is something that only arises through the exchange process. In fact, as will later be discussed, industrial capital depends on the margin (surplus value) that exists in the process of the purchasing of the 'commodity' called labour power and the selling of the commodity thereby produced. Thus, consideration of merchant capital discloses the characteristics of capital in general.

Exchange (buying and selling) is always formed through an agreement or consent between two parties. In principle, unless there is an equality between what is exchanged, exchange itself (buying and selling) does not emerge. Exchange must be seen, at least by the exchangers themselves, as equal. Yet, originally, the distinction between equal exchange and unequal exchange became possible only at the moment when the inherent value of a single commodity was considered. When exchange takes place above or below the inherent value of a single commodity, it is unequal exchange.

However, what we are treating here as the inherent value of a commodity can itself only be posited at precisely the moment when two mutually distinct systems of value-relation come to be thought. The value of a commodity in a single system is simply a relative value determined by multiple relations, and, in this sense, the distinction between equal and unequal exchange is meaningless. Thus, exchange in the interior of this system would never give rise to surplus value. This is what Marx means when he writes, above: 'The capitalist class, as a whole, in any country, cannot over-reach themselves.' Consequently, it is only through the mediation between two differing systems that the existence of unequal exchange or surplus value first becomes a necessity.

4

Saussure destroyed 'meaning' when he grasped language as the value-form. Yet, on the other hand, he speaks of the 'value' of language – not its 'meaning'. For example, the words 'tree' and 'arbor' share a 'meaning', but, within each of their respective systems (*langue*), they hold different relations to other words. This is the point at which their 'value' differs. But what Saussure is truly saying is the following. 'Language' in general does not exist anywhere. One *langue*, itself a differential system, exists in contrast to another *langue*. That is, he rejects the myth of Babel – that, until that point, language had been 'one'. This is because the myth of Babel is one logical product of monotheism, in other words, world money.

For example, Plato pointed out the arbitrariness or ambiguity of the relation between the conceptual and the phonetic, since a concept can be expressed differently in Greek and other languages. What Saussure would eventually call the 'arbitrariness of the sign' has been often understood in this way, but it indicates something quite different. For Plato, the concept exists as something translatable between various national languages, just like money in the commercial world of the Mediterranean in his time. When Saussure uses the term 'arbitrariness', he emphasizes, rather, that each language simply existed from the outset as phonetic difference, and that there is no such thing as a 'concept' that would exceed it.

Marx writes as follows:

> On the other hand, as I have before remarked, the exchange of products springs up at the points where different families, tribes, communities, come in contact; for, in the beginning of civilisation, it is not private individuals but families, tribes, &c., that meet on an independent footing. Different communities find different means of production, and different means of subsistence in their natural environment. Hence, their modes of

production, and of living, and their products are different. It is this spontaneously developed difference which, when different communities come in contact, calls forth the mutual exchange of products, and the consequent gradual conversion of those products into commodities. Exchange does not create the differences between the spheres of production, but brings what are already different into relation, and thus converts them into more or less inter-dependent branches of the collective production of an enlarged society.[6]

In other words, what is presupposed is the coexistence of differential systems: the system is something fundamentally 'for others' or 'with others' (*taitateki na mono*).[7] The state exists as the state only in relation to other states. Philosophers often bring up the concept of intersubjectivity, or collective subjectivity. Culture, for example, is precisely a form of collective subjectivity, and perception itself will differ on the basis of culture. But, in the present context, we would say that a collective subjectivity constitutes a system or institution, thus presupposing other collective subjectivities as its own precondition, and that there exists in a sense no *truly* 'collective subjectivity' capable of collectively overcoming all of these. Or rather, what makes it seem that there is indeed such a truly collective subject is 'world money', which gives rise in the religious context to 'world religion'. 'World money', in this sense, perfectly conceals or covers over the more essential heterogeneity.

At this point, we ought to also think the concept of 'number'. As Marx argues, the general form of value or the money-form makes possible the 'qualitative identity and quantitative

---

6 Marx, *Capital*, 357.

7 [Trans.] This term *taitateki* is quite rare in Japanese, although *taita sonzai* is typically used as the translation for Sartre's concept of *l'être-pour-autrui*. Karatani uses it here to indicate that a linguistic system (or differential system in general) must always be linked to its 'others', and cannot exist without this 'other-facing' aspect.

proportionality' of various commodities. This is precisely the level on which number comes to exist, appearing when it abstracts from qualitative difference and renders it into an identity. Consequently, number too conceals the form of value. For Nietzsche, who radically theorized the suppression of heterogeneity, this could not be overlooked:

> Logic itself rests upon assumptions to which nothing in the world of reality corresponds. For example, the correspondence of certain things to one another and the identity of those things at different periods of time are assumptions pure and simple, but the science of logic originated in the positive belief that they were not assumptions at all but established facts. It is the same with the science of mathematics, which certainly would never have come into existence if mankind had known from the beginning that in all nature there is no perfectly straight line, no true circle, no standard of measurement.[8]

In other words, the expression of quantitative proportionality emerges through the concealment of the value-form.

The value of one commodity in a given system only exists in a relation of value with the other commodities in the system, but when given expression by means of money, it appears quantitatively, as price. The merchant capitalist buys commodities at this price and takes them to another system. There, the commodities are placed into a different relation of value, appearing at a price higher than before. Thus, M–C–M′ (M+ΔM) becomes possible only by means of the differential in value-relations between two systems; thus, despite the fact that both C–M and M′–C (which constitute the surface of the M–C–M′ process) exist as forms of equal exchange, surplus value nevertheless emerges.

---

8 Friedrich Nietzsche, *Human, All Too Human*, trans. A. Harvey (Chicago: Charles Kerr, 1908), 30–1.

Chapter Four

1

The development of a commodity economy liquidated the difference between value systems that were previously regionally isolated, 'socially' connecting global production on a large scale in one clean sweep. Obviously, those regions that, despite their isolation, enjoyed self-sufficiency, were no longer able to function without a relation to the world market, and so became rapidly impoverished and divided in class terms. Production gradually transformed into commodity production, and these regions were enclosed by the commodity economy. But this process was driven by merchant capital's capacity to gain surplus value from the erasure of difference itself.

Industrial capital is only formed through the expansion of the commodity economy and emergence of the world market. In attempting to think capital, we must see this difference as a necessary postulate. After all, for capital, surplus value must be obtained from somewhere.

On this point, we ought to first attempt to think the question of the general rate of profit. While we can say, for the time being, that surplus value and profit in general are similar, the annual rate of profit is substantially different from the rate of surplus value gained in a single investment. Even when the rate of surplus value is low, if the rate of turnover of capital is high the annual profit rate will also be high. (For example, even if the rate of surplus value is high in one cycle, if it can only be done twice in one year, the rate of surplus value will be lower, but with more frequently circulating capital, the rate of profit will be identical.) As a result, the investment of various types of capital tends to be equalized through the annual rate of profit. (Inversely, the investment of capital is constrained by the overall rate of profit.) Capital is thus essentially indifferent to the type of process through which surplus value is obtained; capital is only concerned with the rate of profit. Interest rates are formed in relation to the overall rate of profit. While what Marx calls finance capital, M–M', is fundamentally based on this overall rate of profit, simultaneously capital completes the illusion that it is 'self-expanding', unrelated to any factors external to itself.

It is not only that these forms are established prior to the advent of industrial capital; capitalist production is spurred on and becomes possible within these forms themselves. Consequently, industrial capital, which begins with machinic production, never exists solely on its own, nor can it cover over all other forms of production. In order to expropriate surplus value – without which capital cannot be itself – capital in general need not adhere to a specific form of production.

Thus, speaking generally, surplus value is born on the margin between differing systems of value. With respect to merchant capital, it is obviously the case. However, with respect to industrial capital, we can in fact say the same.

As Marx argues, if we posit a unitary, identical system, surplus value derived from the circulation process M–C–M' could not exist. The surplus value gained by industrial capital emerges from a different exchange process, that is, through M–C ... C'–M'. This is the process whereby the capitalist purchases means of production, raw materials and labour power, and then sells on the product produced by means of these inputs. Here, because means of production or raw materials are simple commodities, we can suppose that surplus value is not produced within this single, unitary system. Therefore, the key lies in this commodity called 'labour power'. Put simply, surplus value here exists in the margin between the value of the labour power purchased by the capitalist, and the value of the products actually produced by the labourer (minus means of production and raw materials). But how does this margin come into existence at this point?

Marx divides surplus value into absolute surplus value and relative surplus value. The former is the surplus value obtained by lengthening the working day, while the latter is the surplus value gained by retaining the working day in its existing form while raising the productivity of labour, thereby indirectly lowering the value of labour power.

For example, at first glance, it seems fully justifiable to say that in the lengthening of the working day, the labourer works beyond the value of his or her labour power, in other words, beyond the socially necessary labour time, and thereby surplus value is obtained. But, if we think carefully about this conception, it immediately falls into difficulty. For instance, when individual capitalists go bankrupt, in one sense it can be taken to mean that they were unable to obtain any surplus value, and thus that they did not adequately 'exploit' their workers. But the reason this sort of sophistry passes as an explanation is that, first, it imagines labour time as a kind of substance, and second, it sees surplus value as something only emerging from the production process.

In Marx's thought, the value of labour power is constituted by the *socially* necessary labour time required for its production. Clearly, this *sociality* is given by means of the money-form, and thus without consideration of the money-form it is impossible to derive the concept of socially necessary labour time. Dividing labour into 'necessary labour' and 'surplus labour', or dividing labour time into 'necessary labour time' and 'surplus labour time', is impossible if limited to the actual production process, requiring us one way or another to theorize the form of value or system of value.

In this sense, the fact that Marx begins his consideration from absolute surplus value, giving numerous concrete examples, frequently invites misunderstandings. The distinction between surplus labour and necessary labour is clear within the feudal mode of production: in this context, it is simple to distinguish between work performed for oneself and work performed for the lord. But, when examining the capitalist system in an analogical manner, we not only lose sight of its specificity, but also become unable to elucidate its mysteries.

In the first place, what characterizes capitalist production is precisely that the distinction between necessary labour and surplus labour becomes impossible. Capitalist production designates a mode within which, at the least, the worker and the capitalist are equal before the law, and insofar as they are contractually in agreement, the worker is not unfairly compelled to work by any kind of external coercion; the payment of the wage that corresponds to the value of their labour (or at least a wage of some sort) is reflected in the consciousness of the worker (and of the capitalist). Thus, there is here an 'equal exchange' at the level of consciousness. Without this aspect, capitalist production would simply be maintained by means of extra-economic coercion, as was the case with the feudal system. The mystery of capitalist production lies in the fact that while it clearly appears to be founded on and characterized by 'equal exchange' at a conscious level, this is not actually the case. Thus, the simplistic and rather commonplace idea that the worker works beyond the level of the wage, a view also commonplace amongst the socialists contemporary to Marx, is incapable of even minimally explaining this mystery. Such a view merely devolves into the political-moralistic slogan of Proudhon – 'property is theft'.

2

Here, there is a crucial reason why Marx begins his argument from the theory of the value-form. The roots of its mysteriousness lie in the fact that, while the value of the commodity is placed within a relational system, it nevertheless is thought to be something that exists as an independent, separate entity. The wage appears to be identical to the value of labour power. But the value of labour power is not something that can exist independently, in separation; it can only come into existence in relation to other commodities.

In capitalist society, labour power becomes a commodity. Or strictly speaking, it is not labour power that becomes a commodity, but the concept of labour power itself – distinct from labour – already comes from the analysis of the commodity form. That labour power could be a commodity is nothing more than a tautology; what is crucial is that the owner of labour power appeared historically.

Marx argues that the precapitalist 'primitive accumulation' gives birth to the following type of labourer:

> For the conversion of his money into capital, therefore, the owner of money must meet in the market with the free labourer, free in the double sense, that as a free man he can dispose of his labour-power as his own commodity, and that on the other hand he has no other commodity for sale, is short of everything necessary for the realisation of his labour-power.[1]

When this doubly free worker emerged, the commodity called 'labour power' was formed for the first time. But this freedom in the double sense holds equally for all commodity owners. Firstly, the commodity possessor does not transfer ownership of his or her possessions to another person outside of exchange. Of course, it is possible to violently dispossess another of his or her products (not commodities). In the feudal

---

[1] Marx, *Capital*, vol. 1 in *MECW*, vol. 35, 179.

system, for example, products are seized by the lord. But insofar as these products are commodities, they at the very least presuppose exchange. The existence of value emerges by means of reciprocity, since the possessions of another cannot be appropriated without exchange. Marx writes, '[The possessors of commodities] must therefore, mutually recognise in each other the rights of private proprietors. This juridical relation, which thus expresses itself in a contract, whether such contract be part of a developed legal system or not, is a relation between two wills, and is but the reflex of the real economic relation between the two.'[2] We ought to say here that in fact, at every historical stage, even in primitive society, exchange is based on mutual consent and contractual forms.

Secondly, the commodity is unnecessary for possessors themselves, and they cannot appropriate the object of desire without its transfer. What can be said of all commodity possessors can be equally said of the possessor of the commodity labour power. In other words, the proletariat is not a human being who possesses nothing, but rather appears simply as one type of commodity possessor. Capitalist society only emerges with the subsumption of labour power as a commodity into the commodity economy as a whole. However, it is not necessary to insert here 'historical conditions', as Marx does. This is because in the expansion of the commodity economy, the doubly free labourer is born as a result of two processes: Protestantism, or bourgeois legal thought, and the enclosures for commodity production. In other words, these all emerge fundamentally by means of 'merchant capital'. Since Marx largely dismissed the analysis of merchant capital, he must insert his specific 'historical conditions'.

At this point, the fact that the proletariat is a commodity possessor becomes decisively important. The value of their commodities stands in a value relation with other commodities.

---

2 Ibid., 95.

Insofar as labour power is a commodity, this is a point simply derived by necessity from the hitherto existing thought. When Marx utilizes the term 'labour time', he uses it to connect labour power and other commodities.

If we follow Marx's point, the value of the commodity consists of the social 'labour time' required for its production, and labour power is no different. Since *social* labour time is first posited by means of the money-form, the substance of Marx's point is simply that labour power exists within a value system in which it depends on relations with all other commodities. When Marx states that the value of labour power differs 'in a given country, at a given period',[3] he implies that we must think the value of labour power as a concept placed within a synchronic system of relation.

3

Thus, how does surplus value become possible? It is simply the margin that exists between the labour power bought by the capitalist, and its products sold thereafter. But here, without considering wage and price, if thought within a synchronic system, the value of labour power and the value of the product correspond to each other, and there is no necessity for a margin or gap to emerge. Merchant capital discovers this margin in the *interval* between different systems, but nothing similar exists in this case. If so, industrial capital, as is often thought in the case of commercial capital, would be simply established through fraud. But all the discussions of being made to work beyond the wage and so forth claim to disclose the 'dark side of the capitalist', while never treating the more fundamental problem of how capital is able to overcome 'human will' and persist. Marx writes as follows:

---

3 Ibid., 140.

> It is therefore impossible for capital to be produced by circulation, and it is equally impossible for it to originate apart from circulation. It must have its origin both in circulation and yet not in circulation. ...
>
> Our friend, Moneybags, who as yet is only an embryo capitalist, must buy his commodities at their value, must sell them at their value, and yet at the end of the process must withdraw more value from circulation than he threw into it at starting. His development into a full-grown capitalist must take place, both within the sphere of circulation and without it. These are the conditions of the problem. *Hic Rhodus, hic salta!*[4]

What is important is that capital, and indeed surplus value, originates in the circulation process and simultaneously in the production process. In other words, it is no longer able to emerge from the circulation between two different systems, as in the case of merchant capital. But neither does capital simply emerge from the production process, because surplus value cannot be formed solely within a single system. So how, exactly, does Marx make this 'leap'?

He does so by conceiving of a production process that itself produces two different systems. This problem cannot be explicated simply by means of absolute surplus value (or the lengthening of the working day). Of course, Marx first speaks of absolute surplus value, and only after does he consider relative surplus value. But this is not a historical order of succession, but simply a logical sequence within Marx's dialectical narrative. In fact, as he will argue later, the lengthening of the working day is only demanded and made possible in the first instance by the presupposition of relative surplus value. The essence of surplus value, which characterizes industrial capital, lies in the category of relative surplus value.

As Marx argues, relative surplus value is born from the increasing productivity of labour. Classical political economy

---

4 Ibid., 176–7.

sought the concept of surplus value in the improvement of productivity through the 'division of labour' and cooperative work. Marx inherited this, calling it 'the new power that arises from the fusion of many forces into one single force'.[5] But, as he argues in three passages from *Capital*:

> The detail labourer produces no commodities. It is only the common product of all the detail labourers that becomes a commodity.[6]

> [The capitalist] pays them the value of 100 independent labour-powers, but he does not pay for the combined labour-power of the hundred. Being independent of each other, the labourers are isolated persons, who enter into relations with the capitalist, but not with one another.[7]

> [The use-value of labour power] consists in the subsequent exercise of its force. The alienation [*Veräusserung*] of labour-power and its real manifestation [*Äusserung*], i.e., the period of its existence as a use-value, are separated by an interval of time.[8]

A rise in the productivity of labour, whether due to an intensification of the division of labour and cooperation, or to technical innovation, will cause a latent reduction in the value of labour power. We could also put it as follows: the capitalist dispatches his or her products into an existing value system despite already producing them cheaply. That is, latently, both the value of labour power and the value of the products are mutually reduced, but this is not immediately actualized. Thus, in this scenario, the currently existing system and the potential system both exist. We discover thereby that industrial capital

---

5 Ibid., 331.
6 Ibid., 360.
7 Ibid., 338.
8 *Das Kapital*, Bd. 1 in *Marx-Engels Werke*, Bd. 23 (Berlin: Dietz, 1962), 188; *Capital*, 184. Translation modified.

too obtains surplus value from the *interval* between two different systems.

We have clarified the process by which merchant capital emerges through the margin between two *spatial* systems of value (although invisible to the persons belonging to them), whereas we might say that industrial capital in this sense, by increasing the productivity of labour, is founded on the creation of *temporally* different value systems.

According to Marx, each individual labourer has no demand to make prior to the emergence of what is produced collectively by means of their 'combination'. Here, there is a temporal relation of before and after that produces an inevitable 'opacity'. Surplus value in industrial capital thus comes not from violence or fraud, but from this sort of inevitable 'unconscious'.

A rise in the productivity of labour creates a latent system within the existing system. Despite the external appearance of equal exchange, a margin or discrepancy is possible. This margin, too, is almost immediately erased, and a value system is formed on the basis of a new standard. Capital ceaselessly creates margins, gaps and differences. In the era of industrial capitalism, an unprecedented velocity of technical innovation became the motivation and condition of its existence.

Certain ideologues glorified the technical revolution, as in the case of the classical political economists, while others opposed it. However, what is most important is neither to praise nor to disparage this technical revolution of industrial capital: what is crucial is to clarify its causes. Capital is preordained not to civilize the world, but to preserve and maintain itself through technical innovation. Seemingly useless technical innovations too are essential to capital's self-preservation. This springs not from any human 'natural' necessity, but from the necessity of the expansion of value.

In addition, to avoid any confusion, we must state unequivocally that a reduction in the value of labour power has nothing whatsoever to do with a reduction in the wage, or impoverishment. It means simply that it has been *relatively* reduced, in relation to the existing system of value. Moreover, this margin or difference is quickly erased. In the newly formed system of value – of course, a relational system – the diminished value of labour power corresponds to the diminished value of its products. As a result, the conditions of existence for the labourer are ameliorated and the working day shortened. There is no contradiction whatsoever between these sorts of improvements in the life of the worker and capital's ability to obtain relative surplus value. If we understand that value is itself always relative value, and surplus value is a relative margin or difference, it becomes clear that the nucleus of capitalist production lies in the creation of a latent system of value, by increasing the productivity of labour.

What I have argued above is that capitalist production essentially originates in the mystery of money itself, which turns difference into identity. Theorizing the capitalist system while ignoring the question of money is meaningless. We cannot give an adequate response to the question: where has capitalist society come from and where is it going? This is precisely because such a question is already mistaken. There is no reason or telos in the process of 'development' that has brought us to capitalist society. Rather, it is the capitalist economy itself that has given these to us. What is seen as 'development' is nothing but a series of inversions accumulated on top of the fundamental inversion called the 'money-form', yet the money-form itself conceals this fact. Not only does the novelty and force of Marx's *Capital* lie in this consideration of the value-form in relation to the 'origin' of money, it also exposes the perspectival perversion (*enkinhōteki tōsaku*) of all 'philosophies of history', including historical materialism.

At this point, we might ask: why was classical political economy unable to discover the value-form? Or, indeed, why did Marx consider the value-form to be the decisive key concept? No Marxian economists have yet supplied an adequate answer to this question. For example, even in the *1844 Manuscripts*, Marx criticizes classical political economy. But, between this criticism and that of *Capital*, there is a crucial difference. Simply put, it is the phenomenon of *crisis*. Insofar as the *1844 Manuscripts* lack any theory of crisis, no matter how much Marx criticized classical political economy, he remained within its framework. Similarly, no matter how much the Young Hegelians criticized Hegel, they could not exit the framework of Hegelianism.

What is important here is that Marx's turn, whether in political economy or in philosophy, took place through the mediation of crisis. Of course, periodic crises already existed. However, although they existed, they were not *perceived*. For classical political economy, these were just exceptional, abnormal circumstances, mere failures of policy. Marx's novelty was to emphasize that rather than abnormalities, these crises are uniquely specific to the capitalist economy. In this, it resembles Freud's novelty: what the hitherto dominant psychology considered an exceptional state – madness – Freud located at the core of the 'human'.

Crisis itself is a kind of rebuke to classical political economy, which saw crisis as a state of exception. To the extent that the capitalist economy functions 'normally', deism in the style of Adam Smith or rationality come to dominate. Crisis itself was born from the interior of the 'rational order' of the eighteenth century. And yet crisis (political and economic)[9] was invisible within their discursive system. Actually existing, and unable to be seen.

When functioning 'normally', the economy appears natural and self-evident. In the blink of an eye, crisis discloses that

---

9 [Trans.] Two terms exist in Japanese for 'crisis' in English and most Western European languages: *kyōkō*, which is specific to economic and financial crises, used in the Marxian sense of 'crisis theory', and *kiki*, which indicates a crisis in a general sense, political, cultural and so forth.

it all was built upon an illusion. Far from being something material, crisis reveals the economy itself as a form of illusion. The perspective that examines the capitalist economy not in its 'normal' aspect but in its 'exceptional' or 'abnormal' aspects was precisely the enabling condition for the radical critique of classical political economy undertaken in *Capital*, and, by developing this discussion not in the field of philosophy proper, Marx also enabled a critique of the totality of the history of philosophy.

Before we argue that crisis requires a theory of the value-form, there is one point that must be made. Marx in the 1850s was clearly a believer in crisis as the harbinger of great revolutionary hopes: he predicted multiple impending crises, expecting these to spark revolution across Europe. As is now well known, none of his predictions were fulfilled. Crisis was less something to be elucidated than it was the one hope left for Marx at the time, living in exile after the failure of the 1848 revolutions. Obviously, this type of theory of crisis-based revolution retains strong roots among contemporary Marxists. But, speaking from historical experience, far from fuelling political revolutions, crises have always worked to the advantage of counter-revolutionary politics, including fascism. Unless we do away with the illusion of crisis as a bridge to revolution, we will remain basically unable to approach the true problematic that crisis poses.

For Engels, crisis is explained in terms of the 'anarchy of production' and the 'contradiction between the social character of production and the private character of appropriation'. But this form of explanation cannot adequately account for the riddle of the regularity of periodically occurring crises. Uno Kōzō criticized this presentation of the problem, theorizing periodic crisis from the contradictions of labour power as a commodity.[10] Unoist theory is unquestionably more

---

10 [Trans.] On Uno's theory of crisis, see Gavin Walker and Ken Kawashima, 'Surplus Alongside Excess: Uno Kōzō, Imperialism, and

consistent, but remains unable to explain why *Capital* treated the theory of the value-form as indispensable. From the outset, to call something labour power means that it is simply a commodity; it is not that 'labour power *becomes* a commodity'. In other words, concealed within the concept of labour power is the money-form. Marx distinguished between labour and labour power, but this distinction merely restates the dualism of value and use-value; the problem, as I have stated before, is that this dualism is itself a product of the money-form. Thus, no matter how much one asserts the importance of this distinction between labour and labour power, it either remains within the framework of classical political economy or leads to a theory of alienation whereby 'labour power becomes a commodity'. When such a perspective proposes that 'the species-being [*Gattungswesen*] of man is alienated', although we ought to accurately define what exactly this 'species-being' is, it is simply treated metaphysically, as given from the outset.

Economists rarely grasp the fundamental problematic of crisis. Certainly, neoclassical economics, practised in abstract laboratory settings – so-called modern economics – cannot even see the problem. Keynes understood crisis or recession as the unique 'illness' of the capitalist system, proposing a course of aggressive treatments of its symptoms. Theoretically, this assessment is superior to the latter-day crisis-as-revolution model. However, my concern here is not to construct a theory of economic crisis, which would require a comprehensive analysis of credit and the business cycle. The question is not why crisis occurs, but rather why the problematic of crisis could become the lever for Marx's critique of classical political economy and Hegelian philosophy, and indeed for his critique of Western metaphysics as such.

Actual crises do not reveal the limits of the capitalist system. In the nineteenth century, crises were simply one form of the

---

the Theory of Crisis', in *Viewpoint 6: Imperialism*, February 2018, viewpointmag.com.

business cycle, and in the latter part of the twentieth century, apparatuses had been formed to somewhat alleviate their danger. As long as we link crisis with revolution, we cannot understand crisis. It is like the situation of psychoanalysis: despite the popularization of psychoanalysis as a form of therapy, the radicality of the problematic detected by Freud in neurosis has rarely been grasped. Today, it is arguably difficult to find anyone who resembles a classical hysteric.

As we should note, the condition Marx called the 'possibility of crisis' is also, in fact, the condition of surplus value. The condition of possibility for capital is the condition of crisis. To put it another way, what renders possible 'normality' also renders possible 'abnormality'. Thus, when the capitalist economy reaches a certain scale, it gives birth to crisis. Michel Foucault argued that in the eighteenth century, for the first time, the figure of the 'madman' was produced, through a structure of selection and inclusion based on 'reason'. Similarly, crisis came to exist in tandem with the establishment of industrial capitalism, which enabled the possibility of classical political economy. In this case, crisis was obviously seen as a state of exception. But whether it was seen as something to be 'treated', or expected, *qua* crisis, to destroy 'rationality', what was never questioned was what had enabled the *existence* of crisis itself. Here the money-form is seen as something self-evidently universal. In planned economies without crises – that is, in those states labelled 'socialist' – the realization of a form of violent control by means of 'reason' has its origins in a Marxism that could only grasp the problematic of crisis in 'economic' terms.

What is crisis? It is the sudden dissolution of a system of value relations. At this point, the inherent value of a thing disappears. In other words, the value-form – the hieroglyphic – previously concealed by the money-form, is revealed. Commodities lose their value. The commodity means merely the commodity-form, not a thing. Even though a thing is right before their eyes, they cannot grasp it. Just like an aphasia sufferer cannot perceive a thing as a thing.

Crisis illuminates the way in which the money-form is established. Marx, just like Freud, returned to the 'infancy' of the capitalist system, turning towards the world of the 'unconscious' that is the value-form.

Chapter Five

1

Since the discovery of the *1844 Manuscripts*, the relation between the 'early Marx' and the 'late Marx' has been problematized on a global scale. To put it simply, the debate has been concentrated on one central point: whether to consider the late period as an extension of the early work, or to view the late Marx through the notion of a 'break' with the earlier period. This is not just a problem of 'Marxology' but has real political significance in the contemporary moment. First and foremost, the emphasis on the early Marx came from an opposition to a Marxism seen to tend towards economic determinism and theories of the development of the productive forces, while emphasis on the late Marx came from a rejection of the theory of alienation, as something reducing Marxism to the level of bourgeois humanism. To restate it in another sense, the early Marx was upheld against Stalinism, while the late, anti-humanistic Marx was upheld against the former's humanism. As always, a strong and forceful Marxism intermingled with its negation, or the negation of its negation, to form a central, critical split in the reading of Marx's texts.

However, this debate only existed within an enclosure of various 'meanings' of Marx's texts. In this sense, the debate itself cast its participants back into the realm of historicism, much like the debates around the concepts of 'the medieval' and 'modernity'. For example, from a certain perspective, Europe in the twelfth century was already modern, while from other perspectives, even the eighteenth century was still fundamentally medieval. So, the debate over pinpointing the advent of modernity remained unproductive, insofar as it did not place into question the era in which the concept of the medieval was created, nor the historicity of modern historiography itself.

The debate over the continuity or rupture between the early and late Marx is much the same: caught in a trap. Once again, prior to *reading* the texts, Marx's 'thought' is presupposed, and this is never questioned. However, as I have shown already, nothing in the text of *Capital* is transparent; on the contrary, what Marx problematized there was precisely 'opacity' itself. Without reading *Capital*, how can one even presuppose a 'late' or 'early' Marx?

'The anatomy of man', writes Marx, 'is a key to the anatomy of the ape.'[1] Let us carefully consider this phrase. The anatomy of the text of *Capital*, into which Marx poured his blood and sweat, is the key to the other texts, and not the other way around. In fact, in *Capital*, Marx does not take up the historicist narrative by which ape evolves into man. The initial commodity that Marx discovers at the outset of the text is not something primordial, stemming from primitive society, but precisely the commodity within capitalist society.

When we earlier took up Marx's doctoral dissertation, *The Difference Between the Democritean and Epicurean Philosophy of Nature*, I read it following a 'reading' of *Capital*. What I refuse is the historicist fiction of Marx's conceptual development, from the dissertation to *Capital*. If *Capital* did not exist, who would even bother reading back to the dissertation? The early Marx is not the origin of *Capital*, but its result. The very originality of this dissertation first becomes clear, not in relation to its meaning within the contemporary context of its writing, but rather through an understanding and reading of *Capital*. What is absolutely crucial about the text known

---

[1] Marx, 'Preface' to *A Contribution to the Critique of Political Economy*, in *MECW*, vol. 28, 42.

as *Capital* is precisely that it problematized the concept of the text itself. For Marx, the commodity (commodity-form) means simply 'text'.

The 'beginning' of Marx's work lies in his reading of the fragmentary texts of Epicurus and Democritus. This was more important than all the 'thought' he acquired the knowledge of in youth, a point that he himself confirmed on more than one occasion in later life. In other words, it is precisely the *problématique* of the text as fragment, the conscious system and the 'internal' system, that constitutes the novelty of Marx's thought. We do not need to, indeed *cannot*, put this into chronological terms. After all, such an attempt would amount to nothing but a *regression* from Marx.

2

The author expresses thought and sensation in the work, and these are received by the reader. Although this is how it appears and how it is typically conceived, it was Valéry who more than anyone disclosed for us the *mystical* character of this problem. For him, it is not just that the work is independent of the author, but more that the work itself creates this thing called 'the author'. It is not just that the thought of the work is something different from the author's ideas, but that it continuously produces an 'author' who possesses such thought. For example, Soseki is an author who has been interpreted and re-interpreted countless times. Whatever the author himself or his acquaintances might say, the fact is that an 'author' exists who has been 'retrojected' from the work, and in fact this 'author' is *all that exists*. The objective figure of Soseki is simply the dominant image created by his readers. In the same sense, no 'true Marx' exists.

Reading is a metamorphosis of the author. A 'true understanding' is impossible, but even if it were, it would bring an end to history, so to speak. In Hegel's aesthetics, as in his philosophy of history, history is brought to its conclusion through a 'true understanding'; this is because his text failed to gain independence through an opacity that can neither be fully grasped nor be overcome by the consciousness of either author or reader.

In his doctoral dissertation, Marx does not begin from the thought of Epicurus (or Epicureanism), but from the texts of natural philosophy seen as more or less similar to the texts of Democritus. The difference between the two, regarded until that point as relatively arbitrary, now undergoes a metamorphosis, placing into relation their 'thought', previously treated as if one had no relation to the other. That is, by deconstructing a certain Epicureanism that had become independent of the text, Marx creates the author called Epicurus. In fact, there is no such thing as 'reading' outside of this type of 'transformational reading' (Merleau-Ponty).

For example, in the doctoral dissertation, Marx does not approach the difference between the two from the 'infrastructure' or 'base'. The uniqueness of his method comes precisely from the fact that Marx himself does not utilize what is widely thought to be the 'Marxist' method. In the dissertation, Marx problematizes the concept of 'infrastructure' or 'base', yet he does not employ the term itself, and never treats it as something 'economic'. However, we should not forget that, when Marx emphasizes the specifically economic base in *The German Ideology*, it is once again derived from a specific textual reading.

As pointed out previously, Marx attempts to deconstruct the space of identity – as old as the history of philosophy itself – that covered over or hid the 'difference' between the Epicurean and Democritean philosophies of nature. In this sense, philosophy means ideology, and in *The German Ideology* constitutes precisely a discovery of the difference that philosophy conceals.

For example, Marx states that the motor-force of history – reason, divine Providence, 'Man', the *Zeitgeist*, and so on – amounts simply to the 'imagined subject'[2] (author) presupposed in the background of history-as-text. In negating this author, or transcendental signified exterior to the text, Marx for the first time discovers the economic 'infrastructure', a theoretical position fundamentally different from a historicist economic history. What is important here is his awareness of the fact that history, narrated as the history of philosophy, always conceals difference under the aspect of universal truth. The concept that leads Marx here is of course 'class', but his conception differs significantly from – or even opposes – the notion of 'class struggle' dominant since the French Revolution:

> If now in considering the course of history we detach the ideas of the ruling class from the ruling class itself and attribute to them an independent existence, if we confine ourselves to saying that these or those ideas were dominant at a given time, without bothering ourselves about the conditions of production and the producers of these ideas, if we thus ignore the individuals and world conditions which are the source of the ideas, we can say, for instance, that during the time that the aristocracy was dominant, the concepts honour, loyalty, etc. were dominant, during the dominance of the bourgeoisie the concepts freedom, equality, etc. The ruling class itself on the whole imagines this to be so. This conception of history, which is common to all historians, particularly since the eighteenth century, will necessarily come up against the phenomenon that increasingly abstract ideas hold sway, i.e. ideas which increasingly take on the form of universality. For each new class which puts itself in the place of one ruling before it, is compelled, merely in order to carry through its aim, to represent its interest as the common interest of all the members of society, that

---

2 Marx, *The German Ideology*, in *MECW*, vol. 5, 37.

is, expressed in ideal form: it has to give its ideas the form of universality, and represent them as the only rational, universally valid ones.[3]

In other words, the ideals that appeared to everyone to be self-evident, i.e., freedom, equality, and so on, exist only insofar as they conceal this class difference. In Marx, the forces and relations of production do not 'explain' history, but rather cover over and conceal history from us. Historical materialism – a phrase never used by Marx himself – emerged by overlooking this point. Historical materialism is a 'meaning' that came to exist in separation from Marx's texts: it is, rather, the 'philosophy' of Engels.

3

Marx wrote the *1844 Manuscripts* in exile in Paris. As is well known, these were systematic considerations of Feuerbach's theory of alienation, expanded into the theory of the state and political economy. The following year, forced to flee to Brussels, Marx wrote the *Theses on Feuerbach* and *The German Ideology*. This turn from 1844 (when he was twenty-six years old) to the following year, what we might call, after Valéry, his 'intellectual coup d'état', is not limited to the transition from devotion to Feuerbach to a critique of Feuerbach. For example, Louis Althusser sees in this moment an 'epistemological break', while Hiromatsu Wataru locates there the influence of Engels. What Althusser and Hiromatsu share is an opposition to the boom in popularity of the theory of alienation, both seeking in *The German Ideology* to ground a historical materialism divorced from Hegelianism in a true sense.

However, Marx wrote his doctoral dissertation under the influence of the Young Hegelian Bruno Bauer, and, although

---

3 Ibid., 60.

he had not yet taken up Feuerbach, he had already developed a unique perspective from which to advance a critique of the history of philosophy, a perspective much more original than simply the materialist inversion of Hegelian idealism. It would be completely arbitrary to try to chronologically prove Marx's 'break' from Hegelian-Feuerbachian forms. In fact, in a certain sense, for his entire lifetime, Marx never really shook off the Hegelian mode of thought; but if there is a point of divergence, it appears already in his distance from the Hegelians in the doctoral dissertation. Viewed from the perspective of something highly general, like the concept of 'alienation', Marx appears as nothing more than a typical Young Hegelian. However, if we take a methodological approach that attends closely to 'the smallest details', as he put it in the doctoral dissertation, the difference between Marx and the Young Hegelians becomes clear. In fact, it is really only within this difference that 'Marx' comes to exist, rather than in any supposedly pure space that declares: 'Here is the true thought of Marx.'

Instead, Marx's 'thought' is located in his method of reading texts. Marx's turn in *The German Ideology* does not stem from the proposal of a new philosophy, but from his deconstructive reading of the ideology called 'philosophy' itself. This turn is not an 'inversion' but a 'movement'. For example, if Marx did not exactly throw away his perspective from the *1844 Manuscripts*, nor did he come to invert it. He simply moved. But what would this mean, concretely?

In *The German Ideology*, he writes from the following place:

> If we wish to rate at its true value this philosophic charlatanry, which awakens even in the breast of the honest German citizen a glow of national pride, if we wish to bring out clearly the pettiness, the parochial narrowness of this whole Young-Hegelian movement and in particular the tragicomic contrast

between *the illusions of these heroes about their achievements* and *the actual achievements themselves*, we must look at the whole spectacle from a standpoint beyond the frontiers of Germany.[4]

This is Marx's view, already exiled from Germany and embedded in the reality of another country. Had Engels written it, it would be one thing, but there is something in Marx's statement above that cannot simply be reduced to sarcastic ridicule: only one year before, he himself had been internal to the 'parochial narrowness' of this 'whole spectacle'. He had just written the *1844 Manuscripts* along Feuerbachian lines. And yet this same Marx suddenly came to criticize Feuerbach, and for this there must have been an internal process that cannot be solely ascribed to his encounter with Engels. In other words, in the above lines of vicious polemic are also concealed the scars borne by Marx himself.

For example, the attempt by Marx and Arnold Ruge to form the *Deutsch–Französische Jahrbücher*, forging a conjunction between German philosophy and the French political movements, was quietly scuppered by the indifference of the French side. It was never likely that theory, formed from the deductive reasoning of philosophy, and French socialism, intuited from direct, actual experience, would find it easy to ally. It was not simply some incompatibility of national consciousnesses, but rather immediate, actual experience that would not allow it. The twenty-six-year-old Marx, young and full of confidence, was surely not only aware that German philosophy itself would not be easily comprehended; he also had to think of the fast-moving reality that seemingly had no link to such theoretical work:

> It has not occurred to any one of these philosophers to inquire into the connection of German philosophy with German

---

4 Ibid., 28. The emphasis is Karatani's.

reality, the relation of their criticism to their own material surroundings.[5]

It had not fully occurred to Marx himself, either. The point is not some kind of banal reasoning to the effect that German philosophy (the superstructure) is determined by its material base and environment. Were that the case, this statement would represent a sort of 'historical materialism' in gestation, but, in Marx, it is something quite different. It is, rather, the self-awareness of a human being whose illusions have been destroyed, who has come to realize that he must ask: what am I, in reality?

In today's perspectivalism, we are used to the idea of examining the world of a certain time, focused on a central figure, in this case Marx. But it is important to emphasize that, far from being 'central', even in his later years, Marx was known merely as the person who had happened to write *Capital*, vol. 1. In truth, we might say it was the stark sense that he was nobody in this world which gave Marx the piercing self-awareness to depart Germany:

> The social structure and the State are continually evolving out of the life-process of definite individuals, but of individuals, not as they may appear in their own or other people's imagination, but as they really are; i.e. as they operate, produce materially, and hence as they work under definite material limits, presuppositions and conditions independent of their will.[6]

The world is not something that can be fully encompassed by a conclusive ideal. No reality exists that can be made to conform to the self-development of an ideal. The theory of alienation, which imagines that human beings are alienated from the various forces of their species-essence and must restore this to themselves, will not hold here. What Marx

---

5 Ibid., 30.
6 Ibid., 35–6.

discovered is the world as a multi-layererd structure, in which the human being both drives and is driven in ways that will not go 'the way we think'. There is no such thing as 'species-essence'. 'But the human essence is no abstraction inherent in each single individual. In its reality it is only the ensemble of the social relations.'[7] That is, the filter of idealism has been removed from Marx's vision, and in it is now reflected the reality, or social relations, in which he himself is caught, a reality that acts regardless of his will. What he discovered is not what we might call the objective world, but the world as an object that exists without regard to our expectations, the world that moves, that refuses to follow our interpretations.

Already, Marx wrote the following in Paris:

> The *maître d'école* describes correctly the condition to which isolation from the outer world reduces a man. For one to whom the *sensuously perceptible world* becomes a *mere idea*, for him mere ideas are transformed into *sensuously perceptible beings*. The figments of his brain assume corporeal form. A world of tangible, palpable ghosts is begotten within his mind. That is the secret of all pious visions and at the same time it is the general form of insanity.[8]

For consciousness, to 'think' is to 'be'. Thus, when a person cannot in fact see how they 'are', they fall into a kind of loss of the external world, wherein 'thinking' is itself 'being', a state precisely of insanity. Minkowski argued that the chief characteristic of schizophrenia was the sensation of being far from the external world, a point that corresponds to Marx's words above.

Of course, the Young Hegelians Marx discusses were not insane *as* individuals. What caused this 'separation from the external world'? It was not the national border, nor was it a lack of interest in the external world. In fact, these libertines

---

7 Marx, *Theses on Feuerbach*, in MECW, vol. 5, 7.
8 Marx, *The Holy Family*, in MECW, vol. 4, 184.

were more progressive than Marx, and more destructive. If Marx could serve as the editor of the *Neue Rheinische Zeitung*, it was because its bourgeois sponsors recognized him as a relative moderate. In criticizing the libertines and French communists, he even appeared, at first glance, to be somewhat conservative.

What Marx was saying was that, no matter how radical they might be, or how realistic and objective, they remained within the dream of self-interpretation. No matter how excessively interested in the external world, still they experienced a fatal loss of awareness of it. We should not forget that Marx was one of them. The crucial point is that, as we will discuss shortly, what separated them from the external world was neither a border nor a psychological disorder, but their linguistic system itself.

4

After he began to see German philosophy from the outside, Marx detected pathological symptoms in its philosophical discourse. What he brought up at this moment was not a 'philosophical' inversion of the 'from idealism to materialism' type. The discourse of philosophy itself was the symptom, whether idealist or materialist. But Marx did not simply view this from outside, from some objective site. As Husserl argued, the concept of objectivity given to us by modern physics depends on the transcendental collective subjectivity that is mathematics. The 'outside' is not some place from which things can be seen objectively, but a site through which the fact that objectivity itself is never anything but a local collective subjectivity, becomes visible. Marx's standpoint is precisely that all 'standpoints' are always uncertain, a place where they are suspended. What brings philosophy into jeopardy is neither negation nor inversion, but this type of 'movement'. We must not forget that this is not the standpoint of 'Marxism' as such. In contrast, when Marxism appears in this 'world' as one possible standpoint, it is in fact a standpoint that decodes the actual meaning of its own discourse.

'The philosophers have only interpreted the world, in various ways; the point is to change it.'[9] Marx argues here that the discourse of philosophy is nothing but 'interpretation'. We should not mistake this for the movement from theory to practice, from the library to the streets. What Marx continually criticizes is the form of 'interpretation' that dominates those who attempt to change the world. To put it otherwise, Marx's work is the interpretation of philosophy itself *as* 'interpretation'. The centrality, universality, transcendence of philosophy itself is the symptom, and what characterizes the work of Marx is the attempt to decode the difference or relationality that it conceals.

At a certain moment, this was called the theory of ideology. However, we cannot, for example, refer to ideology simply as 'false consciousness'. To see ideology as a set of delusions lodged in one's head is to not understand ideology at all. Ideology is, rather, 'true consciousness' or even 'truth' itself; we might say that ideology exists only as 'objectivity'. In other words, ideology is a kind of 'thing'. This is precisely one of the reasons that Marx, in *Capital*, theorizes the 'mysteriousness' of this thing called 'the commodity', and, in this sense, *Capital* itself is a theory of ideology. Rather, if we do not take the vantage point of *Capital*, we will remain unable to understand what ideology is. When we hear 'objective' scientists expound on the 'end of ideology', we should be aware that it is their objectivity itself that has already been reified, and this is precisely Marx's conception of the ideological. As Thomas Kuhn made clear in the field of the history of science, truth is not established on the basis of objective data; it is rather that

---

9 Marx, *Theses on Feuerbach*, 9.

CHAPTER FIVE

the epistemological paradigm which establishes truth itself conversely enables the data to be discovered.

Ideology is thus a 'consciousness of truth'. Marx once wrote to Arnold Ruge, 'This does not mean that we shall confront the world with new doctrinaire principles and proclaim: Here is the truth, on your knees before it! It means that we shall develop for the world new principles from the existing principles of the world. We shall not say: Abandon your struggles, they are mere folly; let us provide you with true campaign-slogans. Instead, we shall simply show the world why it is struggling, and consciousness of this is a thing it must acquire whether it wishes or not.'[10] However, in *The German Ideology*, Marx precisely attempts to 'interpret' the 'will to truth' itself. What he problematizes there is not so much philosophy as the existence of the philosopher. Why is the philosopher a problem? Because the philosopher is an existence (or class) from which the 'will to truth' can never be separated. As Nietzsche argued, within a discourse, what is problematic is not 'what is being spoken' but rather 'who is speaking'. Obviously, it is the philosopher who speaks. But, until this point, no one had problematized the existence of the philosopher as such; the philosopher was hidden within 'truth' or 'essence':

> Hegel himself confesses at the end of the *Geschichtsphilosophie* that he 'has considered the progress of the concept only' and has represented in history the 'true theodicy'. Now one can go back again to the producers of the 'concept', to the theorists, ideologists and philosophers, and one comes then to the conclusion that the philosophers, the thinkers as such, have at all times been dominant in history.[11]

Here, this inverted 'interpretation' of philosophy is detected in the inverted will to power of the philosophers, a point that Nietzsche would later emphasize, but the fact that Marx

---

10 Marx, letter to A. Ruge, September 1843, in *MECW*, vol. 3, 144.
11 Marx, *The German Ideology*, 61–2.

had already taken this perspective was often overlooked. The warped will to power of the 'philosophers' is not something specific only to certain philosophers, but rather belongs uniquely to 'philosophy' itself. We cannot say that idealism represents an inversion but materialism does not. Philosophy itself appears as an inversion of value, whose origin Marx detected in the 'division of labour':

> Division of labour only becomes truly such from the moment when a division of material and mental labour appears. (The first form of ideologists, priests, is concurrent.) From this moment onwards consciousness can really flatter itself that it is something other than consciousness of existing practice, that it really represents something without representing something real; from now on consciousness is in a position to emancipate itself from the world and to proceed to the formation of 'pure' theory, theology, philosophy, ethics, etc.[12]

In Nietzschean terms, this is an inversion (negation) of life by the priest-class, the creation of a value that elevates the inactual over the actual. Here, the decision to problematize the philosopher rather than philosophy comes clear. Within truth, or the essence of the world, is concealed the inverted will of a certain class. The philosopher (priest) remains out of sight, concealed within the value called 'truth'; or, this value itself ascribes value to the philosopher. The 'origin' of philosophy is hidden within its own origin. The signifier that philosophy conceals is none other than the philosopher. Thus, to examine the philosopher is to disclose the secret of philosophy. As Marx states, notions such as the concept, the idea, universality, and so on, begin at the point where they transcendentalize themselves, with the establishment of 'intellectual production' as division of labour. Philosophy, as the 'centre' of various disciplines, was born from centralization – like money. Marx attempts, in the years following *The German Ideology*, to

---

12 Ibid., 44–5.

de-centre philosophy, so to speak. But it is certainly not the case that he simply replaced this centre with political economy.

As we have argued earlier, what is crucial is that Marx read 'class struggle' in midst of discourse, understood as a universal 'truth'. This was qualitatively different from the 'class struggle view of history' that had long pre-existed Marx's intervention. To say that classes exist, and to say that 'class struggle' exists, are completely different statements. For example, in *The German Ideology*, Marx discusses 'feudal or estate property'. However, in this context, class struggle is not something that takes place between aristocrat (or feudal lord) and serf, but between the aristocracy/church and the monarchy/bourgeoisie. Precisely because of this, the establishment of absolutist sovereign rule is the victory of the bourgeois class, and in this sense a thinker like Hobbes, for example, is a typical bourgeois ideologue. Of course, that is not to say that 'struggle' did not take place between lord and peasant; in this context it is mediated by bourgeois ideology in the form of religious reformation.

Class struggle must always and only be apprehended within discourse as universality, as generality. This is why Marx emphasizes that 'the ideas of the ruling class are in every epoch the ruling ideas.'[13] The ruling ideas of our time, those ideas that we find so obvious and self-evident – freedom, equality, humanism – are the ideas of the bourgeois class. Consequently, 'class struggle' itself should only be possible in our time insofar as the fundamental presuppositions of these ideas themselves are called into question.

5

When Marx takes the 'German ideologues' as his interlocutors, philosophy becomes for him a problem. But when it is

---

13 Ibid., 59.

the 'French ideologues' who are in question, the problem is different. The 'French ideologues' with whom Marx engages appear as political factions – practical rather than speculative. For example, what made possible Marx's brilliant explanatory force in *The Eighteenth Brumaire of Louis Bonaparte* was his introduction of an analysis based on the discursive register of the ideologues of this strange political process.

The actual events, occurring from 4 February 1848 to 2 December 1851, appeared to both participants and observers as a mysterious, bizarre dream. But this enigmatic, weird quality stemmed not from any lack of meaning in the events, but from a sort of excess of meaning. What characterized the events is that the 'characters' who appeared on its 'stage' assumed the language and significations of the first French Revolution as their own; not only that, the events themselves converged on the side of an already completed signified. It should be obvious that in order to decipher these events, which reached their final conclusion with the victory of Bonaparte, it was insufficient to simply point to the 'base' or 'infrastructure' as the motor-force of history. We should rather see here the degree to which the political process itself is a site of discourse.

Marx writes at the beginning of the text (and I quote at length):

> Men make their own history, but they do not make it as they please; they do not make it under self-selected circumstances, but under circumstances existing already, given and transmitted from the past. The tradition of all dead generations weighs like a nightmare on the brains of the living. And just as they seem to be occupied with revolutionizing themselves and things, creating something that did not exist before, precisely in such epochs of revolutionary crisis they anxiously conjure up the spirits of the past to their service, borrowing from them names, battle slogans, and costumes in order to present this new scene

in world history in time-honoured disguise and borrowed language. Thus Luther put on the mask of the Apostle Paul, the Revolution of 1789–1814 draped itself alternately in the guise of the Roman Republic and the Roman Empire, and the Revolution of 1848 knew nothing better to do than to parody, now 1789, now the revolutionary tradition of 1793–95. ...

But unheroic though bourgeois society is, it nevertheless needed heroism, sacrifice, terror, civil war, and national wars to bring it into being. And in the austere classical traditions of the Roman Republic the bourgeois gladiators found the ideals and the art forms, the self-deceptions, that they needed to conceal from themselves the bourgeois-limited content of their struggles and to keep their passion on the high plane of great historic tragedy. Similarly, at another stage of development a century earlier, Cromwell and the English people had borrowed from the Old Testament the speech, emotions, and illusions for their bourgeois revolution. When the real goal had been achieved and the bourgeois transformation of English society had been accomplished, Locke supplanted Habakkuk.

Thus the awakening of the dead in those revolutions served the purpose of glorifying the new struggles, not of parodying the old; of magnifying the given task in the imagination, not recoiling from its solution in reality; of finding once more the spirit of revolution, not making its ghost walk again.

From 1848 to 1851, only the ghost of the old revolution circulated.[14]

The ideals, indeed the ghosts, of the past dominated the political factions of the time. They understood their own actions in the present by means of the vocabulary of the past; in this sense, they were dominated by language. More or less the same can be said for the German philosophers. Fiddling around with various Hegelian 'problems', they expanded on

---

14 Marx, *The Eighteenth Brumaire of Louis Bonaparte*, in MECW, vol. 11, 103–5.

a subsection of these in order to return the critique towards Hegel himself: the upshot amounted to little more than a dwarfish, farcical re-enactment of the old master. While the work of Hegel himself, of course, produced extraordinary results, their repetition in the efforts of the Young Hegelians produced vacant, sterile debates with a facade of grandeur. In other words, for the German philosophers, the Hegelian system itself was a 'dead tradition' that 'weighs like a nightmare on the brain of the living'. *The Eighteenth Brumaire* is a masterful satire of Hegel's *Philosophy of History*: in the process from 1848 to 1851, the nephew of Napoleon, whom Hegel had called a 'world-historical individual', rode the waves of this fantasy of the world-historical individual in order to actually seize power, while having not a single aim or ideal to realize. What Hegel conceived of as the 'cunning of history' is here nothing but a farce.

The events took place precisely within their 'language', enclosed within its meaning. We must pay close attention to the fact that Marx's reading of the situation began above all else from this.

The events are narrated beginning on 24 February 1848, with the meeting of the Constituent National Assembly: in other words, from the moment that the February revolution was transferred to the parliamentary power, where for the first time the relation between the 'representatives' and 'the represented' becomes clear. The representatives, that is, the space of discourse, are divided into royalists, Orléanists, republicans, Montagnards, Bonapartists, and so on, while the 'represented' are split into the various relations of production: financial bourgeoisie, industrial bourgeoisie, proletariat, urban petite-bourgeoisie, small-holding peasantry, bureaucrats, lumpenproletariat, and so on.

What Marx emphasizes is the disconnection of the 'representatives' from the interests of the 'represented':

> One must not get the narrow-minded notion that the petty bourgeoisie, on principle, wishes to enforce an egoistic class interest. Rather, it believes that the *special* conditions of its emancipation are the *general* conditions within whose frame alone modern society can be saved and the class struggle avoided. Just as little must one imagine that the democratic representatives are indeed all shopkeepers or enthusiastic champions of shopkeepers. According to their education and their individual position they may be as far apart as heaven and earth. What makes them representatives of the petty bourgeoisie is the fact that in their minds they do not get beyond the limits which the latter do not get beyond in life, that they are consequently driven, theoretically, to the same problems and solutions to which material interest and social position drive the latter practically. This is, in general, the relationship between the *political* and *literary representatives* of a class and the class they represent.[15]

What is once again essential here is that the relationship of conjunction between the 'representatives' and the 'represented' is neither unique nor even necessary:

> The parliamentary party was not only dissolved into its two great factions, each of these factions was not only split up within itself, but the party of Order in parliament had fallen out with the party of Order outside parliament. The spokesmen and scribes of the bourgeoisie, its platform and its press – in short, the ideologists of the bourgeoisie and the bourgeoisie itself, the representatives and the represented – faced one another in estrangement and no longer understood one another.[16]

Precisely because the relation between the 'representatives' and the 'represented' is originally ambiguous, the industrial

---

15 Ibid., 130–1.
16 Ibid., 169–70.

bourgeoisie and other classes overlooked their original 'representatives' and chose instead Bonaparte.

On 24 February 1848, the various parties appeared as 'representatives' – that is, as difference within the location of discourse. Three years later, Bonaparte would seize power as the representative of everything. Marx rejects any sort of explanation that locates this seizure of power in the thought, tactics or personal characteristics of Bonaparte. Whatever perspective one takes is inadequate to explain the mystery of how Bonaparte, who was an utterly meaningless figure in February 1848, could seize power.

At first glance, it looks as if Bonaparte, who appears as the representative of everything, has 'sublated' the opposition between parties and between classes. But this dialectic is negated by Marx. In fact, no 'opposition' existed from the outset – what existed was simple difference. In the first place, an 'opposition' exists between the republicans, royalists, and Orléanists on one side, and the proletariat on the other, but this opposition emerges by means of a transformation of difference into identity. Next, we have the opposition between the republican party and the party of order (the royalists and Orléanists), and after that the opposition between the party of order and the Bonapartists: this frenzy of oppositions continued to proliferate, leading to the final victory of Bonaparte. This process shows us the secret of the 'dialectic' itself (initiated by Plato, systematized by Hegel).

Bonaparte's power was realized through an erasure of difference. At the outset, he was a mere representative of one party-faction, at the end, he was king. Marx states in *Capital* that it is easy to see money in the form of a single commodity, but difficult to see why and how a single commodity should become money. Marx writes as follows on the relation of money and commodity:

> Such expressions of relations in general, called by Hegel reflex categories, form a very curious class. For instance, one man is king only because other men stand in the relation of subjects to him. They, on the contrary, imagine that they are subjects because he is king.[17]

The king (money) appears as the king (money) precisely because he is transcendental, but his transcendental nature is made possible only through the erasure of difference (relation) between parties (commodities). The most difficult theoretical points concerning the theory of the value-form are already expressed in the mysterious passage of Bonaparte from one party-faction to the position of King.

But this inversion has already been theorized by Marx. Although Bonaparte appears as the crystallization of the interests of all parties and all classes, Marx states that he appears as the representative of one class in particular, the small-holding peasantry:

> The small-holding peasants form an enormous mass whose members live in similar conditions but without entering into manifold relations with each other. Their mode of production isolates them from one another instead of bringing them into mutual intercourse. The isolation is furthered by France's poor means of communication and the poverty of the peasants. ...
>
> Insofar as millions of families live under conditions of existence that separate their mode of life, their interests, and their culture from those of the other classes, and put them in hostile opposition to the latter, they form a class. Insofar as there is merely a local interconnection among these small-holding peasants, and the identity of their interests forms no community, no national bond, and no political organization among them, *they do not constitute a class*. They are therefore incapable of asserting their class interest in their own name, whether through a parliament or a convention. They cannot represent

---

17 Marx, *Capital*, vol. 1 in *MECW*, vol. 35, 67 n.1.

themselves, they must be represented. Their representative must at the same time appear as their master, as an authority over them, an unlimited governmental power which protects them from the other classes and sends them rain and sunshine from above.[18]

The small-holding peasantry is a class, and at the same time, not a class. Here is precisely Marx's unique theorization of the concept 'class'. Class does not emerge solely on the basis of a form of economic collectivity or commonality. What allows class to appear as class is something that occurs through discourse, in this case the 'various parties'. Class consciousness means, in this sense, the 'class unconscious'[19] that is only actualized in 'consciousness', that is, in discourse. Marx attempted, in an entirely different sense from the concept of class consciousness in Lukács, to examine the 'conscious' expression of the parties through the structure of their 'unconscious'.

Here, it is legible that the small-holding peasantry, while never directly forming a political party, nevertheless performs the role of one, to render this political process mysterious and dream-like. To be conscious of something is to transform it in language. Since the small-holding peasantry never makes their 'desire' linguistic, when it appears in 'consciousness', that is, in the site of political discourse, it can only appear in inverted form. For the peasantry, Bonaparte is not their 'representative' but their master.

Marx's decoding of the events reads the transcendence of Bonaparte as a 'symptom', through its condensation and dislocation of a 'class unconscious' that is never rendered into language. The rigour of Marx's analysis in *The Eighteenth Brumaire* is absolutely unrelated to any sort of crude determination of the so-called 'base' and 'superstructure'.

---

18 Marx, *Eighteenth Brumaire*, 187–8. The emphasis is Karatani's.
19 See Kenneth Burke, *A Grammar of Motives* (1945) (Oakland: University of California Press, 1969).

Chapter Six

1

I have argued in the preceding pages that Marx, while moving his object of analysis through German philosophy, French political thought, and English political economy, always and each time problematizes the status of *language*. Correspondingly, he moves his point of emphasis. What never changes is his own standpoint, that of the interpreter. From this, Marx's philosophy, political theory and political economy have been derived. But he is neither a philosopher nor a political economist, nor did he establish a new philosophy or new political economy. These are mere silhouettes that remain from Marx's plan to decode the 'interpretation of the world' as discourse: philosophy, political thought, political economy.

For example, in *The German Ideology*, Marx emphasizes the concept of the economic base or infrastructure. He does this precisely because among the German philosophers, materiality was repressed, to put it in a Freudian sense. With regard to a materialist like Feuerbach, Marx writes: 'In *The Essence of Christianity* [*Das Wesen des Christenthums*], he therefore regards the theoretical attitude as the only genuinely human attitude, while practice [*Praxis*] is conceived and defined only in its "dirty-Jewish" form of appearance [*Erscheinungsform*]'.[1]

The German philosophers began as theologians, and, therefore, regarded materiality as something lowly and 'dirty'. For these philosophers, insofar as they thought their own

---

[1] Marx, *Theses on Feuerbach*, in *MECW*, vol. 5, 3.

existence had transcended economic interests, such things merely belonged to the realm of sordid affairs. But in France it was entirely different; there, class struggle was freely discussed. Marx attempts to argue in *The Eighteenth Brumaire* that this type of political discourse in fact concealed the *relations* of production, and in this sense, the base or infrastructure remained economic.

However, in England, such a problem never essentially emerged, since a stark economy actually existed. What Marx turns to is the *discourse of political economy*. In tandem with *Capital*, Marx writes the *Theories of Surplus Value*. The latter is not a historicist research work simply detailing the historical development and relations of influence structuring the theory of surplus value, but, rather, an exposition of the structural transformation and conditions of existence that obtain when one theoretical system (for example, the theory of surplus value held by the Physiocrats) is transferred into another (that of Adam Smith). Marx does not speak here of the 'critique of ideology', but he does develop a critique of the theoretical history of political economy through a focus on its *discourse*.

The fact that Marx treats the English ideologues not via the established duo of philosophy and political thought, but as a discourse concentrated within political economy, amply shows us what he meant by 'ideology'. Ideology does not connote a religious idealism, but, rather, a fact possessing natural self-evidentiary properties, a self-contained, transparent concept (meaning). Here, it becomes possible to re-examine the transcendental concept of 'value' held by classical political economy; it becomes possible to question the hegemony of money/phonetic script, which is precisely what makes this concept of 'value' appear self-evident.

Here it is not that the economic structure is hidden 'below': the problem is, rather, located in explicating the secret of 'concealment' itself. This is why we must pay close attention above

CHAPTER SIX

all to the theory of the value-form. We have to read *against the intentions* of Marx. It is only in doing so that the problematic central to his work comes into relief.

For example, in *The Eighteenth Brumaire*, when Marx points to the hidden structure, it does not mean that the actual political process is simply its shadow. Since the emergence of Marx and Freud, we have grown accustomed to seeing things from the inverse, the reverse, the other side, the underbelly. In other words, it seems that the deep, hidden structure of things is now clear to us. However, it is not that we have suddenly become able to see clearly, but simply that we now construct our reality in accordance with yet another system of meaning. Rather, what we have lost is the ability to see the surface itself.

The Eighteenth Brumaire shows us Marx's dynamic intuition. In examining a political process that has literally just occurred, he is able to casually show us, at the base of a fluid process covered with historical embellishments and full of interconnected, intertwining ideologies, a completely different 'inner structure' than expected. Such a task is impossible for a dogmatic mind; it is unprecedented that the same hand should pull it off more than once. Lévi-Strauss writes, 'Rarely do I tackle a problem in sociology or ethnology without having first set my mind in motion [*vivifié ma réflection*] by re-perusal of a page or two from *The Eighteenth Brumaire of Louis Bonaparte* or the *Critique of Political Economy*.'[2] What he needed was neither Marx's theory nor Marx's method, but a 'setting of the mind in motion'.

Most structuralists treat the insights of Lévi-Strauss as an accepted dogma. They see Marx and Freud as the 'ancestors' of structuralism. Certainly, we cannot deny that Marx discerned an existing system that existed in separation from the 'consciousness' of individuals. What he always emphasized is that human action is, for these humans themselves, always

---

2 Claude Lévi-Strauss, *Tristes tropiques* (Paris: Plon, 1955), 60; *Tristes Tropiques*, trans. John Russell (New York: Criterion, 1961), 61.

subject to a condition of impermeability: but neither did he simply take the 'inner structure' or 'system' as the subject. What Lévi-Strauss calls 'invigoration' (*vivifier*) is something that comes from Marx's vivid mode of seeing and style, intuiting the presence of what at first glance is absent.

Once again, Marx's texts are not to be read as the simple elaboration of a theory; we rather ought to read them for the theory that is implied by the textual object itself. Marx writes:

> For the rest, in respect to the phenomenal form, 'value and price of labour', or 'wages', as contrasted with the essential relation manifested therein, viz., the value and price of labour-power, the same difference holds that holds in respect to all phenomena and their hidden substratum. The former appear directly and spontaneously as current *forms of thought*; the latter must first be discovered by science. Classical Political Economy nearly touches the true relation of things, without, however, consciously formulating it. This it cannot, so long as it sticks in its bourgeois skin.[3]

When he writes in this manner, Marx remains within the Hegelian or Platonic metaphysics of the dichotomy between phenomena and essence. But he is not arguing 'here is essence, here is truth'. Rather, his argument is precisely that the dichotomy of 'phenomena and essence' is something derivative, a product of *money*. Despite his metaphysical use of language, what Marx attempts to assert in the theory of the value-form is that the fundamental 'relation' or difference has already vanished from sight in the 'form of thought' of phenomena and essence. When he uses the phrase 'current forms of thought', what he means is metaphysics. This is, so to speak, the form of consciousness in which the money-form appears as something self-evident and natural, and thus economics (the 'bourgeois skin'), which takes money as its axiomatic or

---

3 Marx, *Capital*, vol. 1 in *MECW*, vol. 35, 542. The emphasis is Karatani's.

tacit presupposition, is forced into a fundamental blindness. Here, the task of *Capital* consists in the discovery of this hidden fundamental difference, and the explication of why it was hidden in the first place. Marx speaks of the 'inner structure' of capitalist society as its 'essence' but it is nothing of the sort. That is, it is not hidden in the background, interior, or depths of the 'phenomena'. Rather, what created these very things themselves is the money-form as centralization. The commodity appears as if it possesses various internal 'values', but these themselves are nothing more than a metaphysics posited by the money-form. It is not that at the foundation of the commodity, there is value. The foundation itself is radically absent, and what is there is the play of the signifier.

2

Seen from this vantage point, it is clear that the *1844 Manuscripts*, under the influence of Feuerbach, presupposed this dualism of 'essence' and 'phenomena'. Later, Marx will write that species-being does not exist, that it is nothing more than the totality of social relations. We might rephrase this and say that the very term 'human' conceals and covers over 'relation' itself. But, if we read this question not in the broad framework of thought in general, but in the 'the smallest details' of difference, even in the *1844 Manuscripts*, Marx's uniqueness clearly exists already. Obviously, it does not lie in the 'theory of alienation', but in what Marx highlighted under the name of 'suffering' and the 'passional':

> To be *sensuous*, that is, to be really existing, means to be an object of sense, to be a *sensuous* object, to have sensuous objects outside oneself – objects of one's sensuousness. To be sensuous is to *suffer*.
>
> Man as an objective, sensuous being is therefore a *suffering* being [*leidendes*] – and because he feels his suffering [*Leiden*],

a *passionate* being [*ein leidenschaftliches Wesen*]. Passion is the essential power of man energetically bent on its object.[4]

This is clearly an argument that bears similarity to Feuerbach, but what distinguishes Marx here is his assertion that man is a 'suffering, passionate being', that he conceives of man as an entity characterized by a fundamental lack in more concrete terms. What is this 'suffering'? An animal too 'lacks', and works passionately in relation to the object, so Marx must mean here something different by 'suffering'. Later, he will write:

> Hunger is hunger, but the hunger gratified by cooked meat eaten with a knife and fork is a different hunger from that which bolts down raw meat with the aid of hand, nail and tooth.[5]

Human 'hunger' is always-already covered in meaning (value). As Lévi-Strauss wrote in *The Raw and the Cooked*, the cooked already belongs to the dimension of culture. Thus, what is in question here is not a lack in the style of the animal's hunger, but a lack that creates meaning itself. In this sense, to 'suffer' should be understood precisely as rooted in the ground of consciousness, culture and history.

One thinker who consistently understood Marx's ontological grasp of this peculiar relation – suffering and therefore passional, active-subjective in order to be passive – was Tanaka Kichiroku.[6] What is it that makes the lack or desire possessed by humans become itself human, or cultural, and

---

4 Marx, Ökonomisch-philosophische Manuskripte, in *Marx-Engels Gesamtausgabe*, Abt. I, Bd. 2 (Berlin: Dietz, 1982), 409; *Economic and Philosophical Manuscripts*, in MECW, vol. 3, 337. Translation modified.

5 Marx, *Economic Manuscripts of 1857–58*, in MECW, vol. 28, 29.

6 [Trans.] Tanaka Kichiroku (1907–1985) was the Japanese translator of the *1844 Manuscripts*, and a major Marxist thinker of the 1950s and 60s in particular, becoming widely influential among the 1968 generation.

where can this be located? As Tanaka observed, Marx located this in the 'physical organization' of the human being:[7]

> The first premise of all human history is, of course, the existence of living human individuals. Thus, the first fact to be established is the physical organisation of these individuals and their consequent relation to the rest of nature. Of course, we cannot here go either into the actual physical nature of man, or into the natural conditions in which man finds himself – geological, hydrographical, climatic and so on. The writing of history must always set out from these natural bases and their modification in the course of history through the action of men.
>
> Men can be distinguished from animals by consciousness, by religion or anything else you like. They themselves begin to distinguish themselves from animals as soon as they begin to produce their means of subsistence, a step which is conditioned by their physical organisation. By producing their means of subsistence men are indirectly producing their actual material life.[8]

Tanaka pointed out in this regard the importance, in biological history, of the category of hairlessness to the conditions of human 'physical organization'. But, if we want to think of this concretely, we must investigate at the general level the human condition as that of the 'naked ape' (Desmond Morris).

In other words, to put it in general terms, the characteristic of human physical organization is lack of instinct – the lack of a mechanism that automatically regulates adaptation to the external environment. Specifically, human suffering emerges through one form of *deferral*. In biological terms, for example, humans go through an unusually long period of infancy. Freud saw in this the reason that generational relations (the

---

7 See Tanaka's *Marukusu, sai-shuppatsu* (Marx: A New Beginning) (Tokyo: Sankōsha, 1980).
8 Marx, *The German Ideology*, in MECW, vol. 5, 31.

relation of parent and child) develop into institutions (the non-natural). This is why he distinguished rigorously between 'instinct' (*Instinkt*) and 'drive' (*Trieb*). 'Drive' emerges from lack; it is already a form of representation, of the signifier. The roots of signification lie in the drive. Here, we should conceive of what Marx calls 'passionate being' precisely in this sense, as the drive itself.

When Marx treats 'the physical organisation of these individuals and their consequent *relation* to the rest of nature' as the first premise of history, what we need to pay attention to is this concept of 'relation'. In other words, this 'relation to the rest of nature' is a form of relation born from a certain lack/deferral, and in fact, it is this lack/deferral that itself is relation as such. After his discussion of language, Marx writes as follows:

> Where there exists a relation, it exists for me: the animal does not enter into 'relations' with anything, it does not enter into any relation at all. For the animal, its relation to others does not exist as a relation. Consciousness is, therefore, from the very beginning a social product, and remains so as long as men exist at all.[9]

In typical speech, animals also have objects, and relate to objects. But, insofar as the animal is inseparable from the environment as a whole, neither object nor relation can exist. Objects and relations only come to exist in deferring/differing. That is, the object-thing is formed in lack/representation (signification).

For example, Susanne Langer locates the distinction between human and animal in the difference in the formal nature of their systems of transmission. The animal possesses a 1-to-1 'response relation' structured only by the sign, while the human possesses a multivocal response relation centred

---

9 Ibid., 44.

on the symbolic. In Marx's terms, a '1-to-1 response relation' is not a relation at all. 'Relation' as such is always multiply layered. The symbolic must be theorized from the standpoint of 'physical organization' subject to deferral.

3

Common to Marx, Nietzsche, and Freud is that they all begin their inquiry from the lack or impotency in 'physical organization' and locate there the emergence of representation, desire, language. This type of perspective can be arrived at from genetic philosophy and likewise from a phenomenological retrospection. As Saussure always reminded us, language is a differential system. That is, meaning is born from the relation of one word (signifier) to another word (signifier). The fundamental roots of signification emerge precisely from this type of spacing. To borrow Jacques Derrida's term, it is precisely what he called *différance* – differing/deferring, from which time and space themselves emerge.

But we cannot ask what produces this *différance* itself. If we do, God or Nature will be simply represented as 'subject', as 'cause'. But this remains a form of 'meaning'; it is not the fundamental origin of signification, but its *result*. What is important is not this type of questioning of 'origin' – itself leading to metaphysics – but rather Marx's point, that human consciousness or 'meaning' does not exist a priori, but only comes to exist in sensuous suffering (passivity).

We should recall here that Marx sought the roots of 'self-consciousness' in the contingency or deviation of the movement of atoms in Epicurus's philosophy of nature. That is, human freedom and subjectivity is not the cause but the result. What lies at the root is the 'deviation' or differentialization of nature itself, or the play of relation of the signifier. Meaning is born from its 'interval' or 'betweenness' (*aida*).

But where this fundamental ambiguity is repressed is the site of the taboo, the institution, the system, and thus 'meaning' or 'consciousness' come to be treated like something *causa sui*, something self-generating and transcendental. Indeed Marx never gave up, throughout his career, this 'natural-historical' mode of understanding:

> To prevent possible misunderstanding, a word. I paint the capitalist and the landlord in no sense *couleur de rose*. But here individuals are dealt with only in so far as they are the personifications of economic categories, embodiments of particular class-relations and class-interests. My standpoint, from which the evolution of the economic formation of society is viewed as *a process of natural history*, can less than any other make the individual responsible for relations whose creature he socially remains, however much he may subjectively raise himself above them.[10]

Here, what Marx calls his natural-historical standpoint is not at all the same thing that Vico, for instance, discussed in terms of the distinction between 'natural history' and 'human history'. Rather, Marx intends by this to emphasize that the 'deviation' of nature itself makes the human an historical being and at the same time, an intentional-passional being. He is not arguing that the human being is a subject and nature is a subject; at the root, he discovers this play of deviation. Or perhaps, more essentially, he discovers that the root or foundation is itself absent.

Marx's perspective above is at first glance a structuralist one, and the structuralists themselves have tended to think so. But Marx's mode of understanding does not simply end with the dispersal of the human subject into its 'location', or into a system of relation without a centre. Rather, the problem is

---

10 Marx, 'Preface to the First German Edition', *Capital*, 10. The emphasis is Karatani's.

not the system of relation as such, but the *systematicity* of the system, a 'preconscious' (Freud) institutionality. This is why he had to write a theory of the value-form.

4

In a 'misunderstanding' that Marx feared, Marxism has largely emphasized the primacy of the teleological consciousness and subjectivity of the human being. In Marx, the 'telos' is to redeem lack, yet also to 'restore' it to *excess*. Thus, 'telos' here always indicates a reversal of deferral. For instance, if we say that we have eyes *in order to* see, this is an example of teleological thought. These typical 'forms of thought' are linked to metaphysics. Nietzsche called this a perversion of perspective in cognition, but it is precisely how teleology in general is established.

On the subject of human labour, Marx writes as follows:

> We presuppose labour in a form that stamps it as exclusively human. A spider conducts operations that resemble those of a weaver, and a bee puts to shame many an architect in the construction of her cells. But what distinguishes the worst architect from the best of bees is this, that the architect raises his structure in imagination before he erects it in reality. At the end of every labour-process, we get a result that already existed in the imagination of the labourer at its commencement. He not only effects a change of form in the material on which he works, but he also realises a purpose of his own that gives the law to his modus operandi, and to which he must subordinate his will. And this subordination is no mere momentary act. Besides the exertion of the bodily organs, the process demands that, during the whole operation, the workman's will be steadily in consonance with his purpose. This means close attention. The less he is attracted by the nature of the work, and the mode

in which it is carried on, and the less, therefore, he enjoys it as something which gives play to his bodily and mental powers, the more close his attention is forced to be.[11]

Certainly, it appears as if Marx here emphasizes that the life of a human being is always teleological, and formed through representation. But to say that the human being has this sort of 'ability' is, paradoxically, also to say that the human lacks the ability of the spider or the bee. As Marx argues in *The German Ideology*, human beings have history because each of them must produce their own means of life within a definite mode of production, something that is conditioned by physical organization. 'Representation' and 'telos' do not exist a priori for the human being; they come to exist through lack and deferral.

However, over the history of Marxism, this teleological consciousness came to be foregrounded. For Lenin, socialism is the sublation of the anarchic capitalist economy, placing under conscious control the totality of society as 'one great factory'. This is just an extension of the attitude of the capitalist inside the factory system. The impermeability that enables the existence of the capitalist is not something 'anarchic'. Let us recall the following point of Marx on the roots of relative surplus value: '[The use-value of labour power] consists in the subsequent exercise of its force. The alienation [*Veräusserung*] of labour-power and its real manifestation [*Äusserung*], i.e., the period of its existence as a use-value, are separated by an interval of time.'[12] After each individual labourer sells his or her labour power, he or she cannot demand payment for those things produced by means of the division of labour and cooperation. Each is individually contracted; there is literally no 'they' that exists at this point in time.

---

11 Marx, *Capital*, 188.
12 *Das Kapital*, Bd. 1 in *Marx-Engels Werke*, Bd. 23 (Berlin: Dietz, 1962), 188; *Capital*, 184. Translation modified.

In other words, what makes relative surplus value possible is this type of temporal gap or slippage, which cannot be controlled by means of teleological consciousness. Yet Marxism forms itself on this basis. For example, Engels writes:

> With the seizing of the means of production by society, production of commodities is done away with, and, simultaneously, the mastery of the product over the producer. Anarchy in social production is replaced by systematic, definite organisation. The struggle for individual existence disappears. Then for the first time man, in a certain sense, is finally marked off from the rest of the animal kingdom, and emerges from mere animal conditions of existence into really human ones. The whole sphere of the conditions of life which environ man, and which have hitherto ruled man, now comes under the dominion and control of man who for the first time becomes the real, conscious lord of nature because he has now become master of his own social organisation. The laws of his own social action, hitherto standing face to face with man as laws of nature foreign to, and dominating him, will then be used with full understanding, and so mastered by him. Man's own social organisation, hitherto confronting him as a necessity imposed by nature and history, now becomes the result of his own free action. The extraneous objective forces that have hitherto governed history pass under the control of man himself. Only from that time will man himself, with full consciousness, make his own history – only from that time will the social causes set in movement by him have, in the main and in a constantly growing measure, the results intended by him. It is humanity's leap from the kingdom of necessity to the kingdom of freedom.[13]

In contrast, Marx cautions: 'But it nonetheless still remains a kingdom of necessity. Beyond it begins that development of human energy which is an end in itself, the true kingdom of

---

13 Engels, *Anti-Dühring*, in *MECW*, vol. 25, 270.

freedom, which, however, can blossom forth only with this kingdom of necessity as its basis.'¹⁴ Of course, the difference between Marx and Engels is crystal-clear: when Marx states the above, he is emphasizing this figure of human existence as 'suffering'.

There is nothing more misguided than the idea of counterposing Marx's supposed humanism to Stalinism. The violence and inhumanity of Stalinism does not come from the repudiation of human subjectivity, but from precisely the reverse, from an absolutization of the figure of the human subject. This position has its roots in Marxism itself, and becomes unavoidable as soon as the point of departure is taken to be the transcendental character of 'consciousness' and 'meaning', a position long ago staked out in Plato's *Republic*. Marxist authoritarianism is a derivation from the tradition of Western metaphysics and religion; I read Marx as someone attempting to deconstruct this tradition. Read any other way, Marx's texts will always necessarily invite the Stalinist reading. We must keep in mind, however, that Marx always emphasizes the perspectival perversion that exists in human teleology and subjectivity:

> It is not a question of what this or that proletarian, or even the whole proletariat, at the moment *regards* as its aim. It is a question of *what the proletariat is*, and what, in accordance with this *being*, it will historically be compelled to do.¹⁵

> Communism is for us not a *state of affairs* which is to be established, an *ideal* to which reality [will] have to adjust itself. We call communism the *real* movement which abolishes the present state of things. The conditions of this movement result from the premises now in existence.¹⁶

---

14 Marx, *Capital*, vol. 3 in MECW, vol. 37, 807.
15 Marx, *The Holy Family*, in MECW, vol. 4, 37.
16 Marx, *The German Ideology*, 49.

CHAPTER SIX

> If men relate their products to one another *as values* insofar as these objects count as merely *objectified husks* of homogeneous human labour, there lies at the same time in that relationship the reverse, that their various labours only count as homogeneous human labour when under *objectified husk*. They relate their various labours to one another as human labour by relating *their products to one another as values*. The personal relationship is concealed by the *objectified* form. So just *what* a value is does not stand written on its forehead. In order to relate their products to one another as commodities, men are compelled to equate their various labours to abstract human labour. They do not know it, but they do it.[17]

> The working class did not expect miracles from the Commune. They have no ready-made utopias to introduce *par décret du peuple*. ... They have no ideals to realize, but to set free the elements of the new society with which old collapsing bourgeois society itself is pregnant.[18]

Marx insisted that to spontaneously define a 'problem' is something fundamentally passive: 'Mankind inevitably sets itself only such tasks as it is able to solve.'[19] However, this is not at all to emphasize the idea, beloved of the structuralists, that the human being is 'coerced' by certain structures. Structure, whether that of the household or of language, can only itself be grasped *teleologically*, and we must now problematize this point. Here there is a delicate, complicated difference.

Teleological consciousness itself emerges from suffering based on deferral. We do not notice this fact when human consciousness exists as spontaneity or subjectivity. And yet, since 'they do not know it, but they do it', it is *doing something*

---

17 Marx, First German Edition of *Capital*, in A. Dragstedt, *Value: Studies by Karl Marx* (London: New Park Publications, 1976), 33.

18 Marx, *The Civil War in France*, in MECW, vol. 22, 335.

19 Marx, 'Preface' to *A Contribution to the Critique of Political Economy*, in MECW, vol. 29, 263.

different from what the human being is 'thinking'. Revolution does not mean to create something new: it means to catch up with the 'transformation' already occurring. When the human being turns to face his or her situation intentionally (teleologically), it is really an attempt to *excessively* retrieve or win back one's 'lateness' or 'delay'.

However, we should never confuse this suffering with the Christian form of the concept. It is instead the concept central to Greek tragedy. If such 'pain' is not something to be relieved or healed, nor is it the concept of 'original sin'. This is because, in the end, it is nothing more than the originary 'deviation' or 'play'.

Chapter Seven

1

In *The German Ideology*, Marx observes the situation of German philosophy from the 'outside'. But the 'outside' here is not simply the physical exterior of Germany. For instance, Marx writes as follows:

> German criticism has, right up to its latest efforts, never left the realm of philosophy. It by no means examines its general philosophic premises, but in fact all its problems originate in a definite philosophical system, that of Hegel. Not only in its answers, even in its questions there was a mystification. This dependence on Hegel is the reason why not one of these modern critics has even attempted a comprehensive criticism of the Hegelian system, however much each professes to have advanced beyond Hegel. Their polemics against Hegel and against one another are confined to this – each takes one aspect of the Hegelian system and turns this against the whole system as well as against the aspects chosen by the others. To begin with they took pure, unfalsified Hegelian categories such as 'substance' and 'self-consciousness'; later they secularised these categories by giving them more profane names such as 'species', 'the unique', 'man', etc.[1]

What made Marx aware of this was a heterogeneous linguistic system in which German philosophy did not compute. When Marx writes, 'This "alienation" (to use a term which will be

---

[1] Marx, *The German Ideology*, in MECW, vol. 5, 28–9.

comprehensible to the philosophers)',[2] by 'the philosophers' he means precisely the German philosophers, suggesting that he already saw and theorized things from a place where the term 'alienation' had ceased to function.

Marx's style begins to noticeably change after *The German Ideology*: if a thinker changes, their style follows suit. If the theoretical content changes, but the style remains the same, it is no real change at all. To break with Hegel is to break with Hegelian terminology. Heinrich Heine, who Marx was personally close to in Paris, displayed a style alien to the Young Hegelians in his *On the History of Religion and Philosophy in Germany*. For the 'European' Heine, who had long been in Paris, German-style philosophical language appeared generally ridiculous. As it did to Marx. But this is not to say that they engaged in an elevation of French thought or regarded it as somehow superior.

The important point is that Marx's break with Hegelian philosophy went hand in hand with an abandonment of Hegelian vocabulary. For example, the term 'alienation' itself, central to Hegel's 'problematic', remained completely internal to Hegel, despite a Feuerbachian inversion. Even today, we can produce innumerable examples of thinkers attracted principally to the *1844 Manuscripts* who are inevitably swallowed up by Hegelian thought. What we must be vigilant about is language. It is not *we* who think, but language that makes us think: this is Marx's understanding in *The German Ideology*. But we must bring this conception further.

Simply to be in another country is already something significant. Regarding Descartes, who lived and thought in the Netherlands, Valéry writes as follows: 'In the philosophical profession, what is essential is not understanding. No matter what star he fell from, he is an eternal foreigner. The philosophers must be shocked by the most commonplace and simple

---

2 Ibid., 48.

affairs.'³ But what Valéry misses here is that, in the first place, Amsterdam in the Netherlands was the most developed and advanced industrial city of the age. The qualitative hierarchy of the mediaeval world view is now just an "expansion", which was not to Descartes' surprise, enabled by industrial civil society. Another 'eternal foreigner', seemingly shocked by that 'most commonplace and simple affair' known as the commodity, would, as we know, go on to radically overturn that older worldview.

Secondly, Valéry fails to see that the 'cogito', in Descartes's terms, is precisely the concept of the grammatical subject in Indo-European languages. When Nietzsche writes the following, he locates in the grammatical system certain tendencies that permeate the whole of Western philosophy:

> That the separate philosophical ideas are not anything optional or autonomously evolving, but grow up in connection and relationship with each other, that, however suddenly and arbitrarily they seem to appear in the history of thought, they nevertheless belong just as much to a system as the collective members of the fauna of a continent – is betrayed in the end by the circumstance: how unfailingly the most diverse philosophers always fill in again a definite fundamental scheme of possible philosophies. Under an invisible spell, they always revolve once more in the same orbit, however independent of each other they may feel themselves with their critical or systematic wills, something within them leads them, something impels them in definite order the one after the other – to wit, the innate methodology and relationship of their ideas. Their thinking is, in fact, far less a discovery than a re-recognizing, a remembering, a return and a homecoming to a far-off, ancient common household of the soul, out of which those ideas formerly grew: philosophizing is so far a kind of atavism of the

---

3 Paul Valéry, 'The Return from Holland', in *Collected Works of Paul Valéry*, vol. 9, ed. Jackson Matthews (Berlin: De Gruyter, 2017).

highest order. The wonderful family resemblance of all Indian, Greek, and German philosophizing is easily enough explained. In fact, where there is affinity of language, owing to the common philosophy of grammar – I mean owing to the unconscious domination and guidance of similar grammatical functions – it cannot but be that everything is prepared at the outset for a similar development and succession of philosophical systems, just as the way seems barred against certain other possibilities of world-interpretation. It is highly probable that philosophers within the domain of the Ural-Altaic languages (where the conception of the subject is least developed) look otherwise 'into the world', and will be found on paths of thought different from those of the Indo-Germans and Muslims, the spell of certain grammatical functions is ultimately also the spell of physiological valuations and racial conditions. – This much by way of rejecting Locke's superficiality with regard to the origin of ideas.[4]

From the perspective of the Japanese language, for example, belonging to what Nietzsche calls the 'Ural-Altaic' languages, we can easily imagine how difficult it is for Westerners to try to escape the structure of the subject. That comes, in a sense, from its inverse: the experience of modern Japan and its relentless attempt to establish the subject – both grammatically (*shugo*) and in practice (*shutai*).[5] In the grammatical

---

4 Friedrich Nietzsche, *Beyond Good and Evil*, in *The Complete Works of Friedrich Nietzsche*, vol. 8, trans. A. del Caro (Stanford: Stanford University Press, 2014), 22–3.

5 [Trans.] The point that Karatani makes here related to the concept of 'subject' in the Japanese language is a long-developed and complex problem for modern Japanese philosophy, criticism, literature and politics. Modern Japanese utilizes at least three (but also, in a sense, many more) terms for the all-encompassing concept of 'subject': *shugo* (the grammatical subject of a sentence), *shukan* (the epistemological subject), *shutai* (the subject of practice, in the sense of 'subjectivity', or *shutaisei*). Further, in a practical sense, the Japanese language itself does not require the constant presence of the subject of

structure of Western languages, in which the subject possesses a violent force of restriction, a sentence without a subject is difficult to imagine: it is always haunted by this structure in which the predicate (or signifier) takes precedence over the subject (or signified).

To put it another way, the English verb 'to be' presupposes within itself both logic and ontology as something natural or self-evident. For example, in English we can transform 'the dog runs' into 'the dog is running', resulting in an interposition or mediacy of 'being' in every event or action, and the same logical judgment appears when 'is' is taken as the copula, as in 'the dog is an animal'. We might say that due to the grammatical peculiarities of Western languages, logic and ontology have made inevitable the sphere of Western metaphysics. However, seen from the perspective of the 'metaphysics of money', this is in no way a problem limited solely to the West.

For example, in classical political economy, 'the value of commodity A *is* this or that.' Thus, value is conceived of as essence (being). In contrast to this, Marx re-imagines the problem as follows: 'The use-value of commodity B signifies the value of commodity A.' Here, 'being' is transformed into 'relation' and use-value as signifier takes precedence over value. What I am calling here the 'metaphysics of money' means that it is the money-form that itself makes 'relation' into 'being'. What Marx attempted to do on this point is different from a simple inversion of subject and predicate.

In the Afterword to the Second German Edition of *Capital*, Marx famously writes:

---

the sentence. In a sense, it is already a different linguistic system from one centred on the subject. That very lack or slippage has significantly conditioned the 'search for a subject' so common to all modern nation states, which require a 'national subject' as the ground of the modern nation. What Karatani intends to indicate here is not the culturalist notion that Japan is somehow always-already outside the problem of Western metaphysics centred on the subject, but precisely the opposite.

> My dialectic method is not only different from the Hegelian, but is its direct opposite. To Hegel, the life process of the human brain, i.e., the process of thinking, which, under the name of 'the Idea', he even transforms into an independent subject, is the *demiurgos* of the real world, and the real world is only the external, phenomenal form of 'the Idea'. With me, on the contrary, the ideal is nothing else than the material world reflected by the human mind, and translated into forms of thought.
>
> The mystifying side of Hegelian dialectic I criticised nearly thirty years ago, at a time when it was still the fashion. But just as I was working at the first volume of *Das Kapital*, it was the good pleasure of the peevish, arrogant, mediocre epigones who now talk large in cultured Germany, to treat Hegel in same way as the brave Moses Mendelssohn in Lessing's time treated Spinoza, i.e., as a 'dead dog'. I therefore openly avowed myself the pupil of that mighty thinker, and even here and there, in the chapter on the theory of value, coquetted with the modes of expression peculiar to him. The mystification which dialectic suffers in Hegel's hands, by no means prevents him from being the first to present its general form of working in a comprehensive and conscious manner. With him it is standing on its head. It must be turned right side up again, if you would discover the rational kernel within the mystical shell.[6]

However, Hegelian logic (ontology) cannot be overcome simply inverting the subject and predicate. What makes the critique of the Hegelian system fraught with difficulty is the fact that it exists as the representative of a Western metaphysics begun by Plato. Certainly, Marx inverted Hegel, but that is precisely where the difficulty started. It goes without saying that the dialectic is a logic formed through the subject and predicate, but merely saying that the predicate becomes the subject is meaningless. What we ought to question instead is

---

6 Marx, 'Afterword to the Second German Edition', in *Capital*, vol. 1 in *MECW*, vol. 35, 19.

the original binary itself of subject and predicate, signified and signifier.

For instance, when Marx emphasizes this idea that 'the use-value of commodity B signifies the "value" of commodity A', a non-existent 'value' has already appeared. Thus, in this expression itself, value as signified is presupposed in advance. If we are to make Marx's theory of the value-form something truly capable of deconstructing the Hegelian dialectic, it cannot simply invert the subject and predicate, but must be read as a question of the 'origin' from which this structure of subject and predicate is itself derived. That is, we must read something that we have not yet thought – Heidegger. He writes, apropos of Nietzsche, and I quote at some length:

> Nietzsche's philosophy, according to his own testimony, is inverted Platonism. We ask: in what sense does the relation of beauty and truth which is peculiar to Platonism become a different sort of relation through the overturning?
>
> The question can easily be answered by a simple recalculation, if 'overturning' Platonism may be equated with the procedure of standing all of Plato's statements on their heads, as it were. To be sure, Nietzsche himself often expresses the state of affairs in that way, not only in order to make clear what he means in a rough and ready fashion, but also because he himself often thinks that way, although he is aiming at something else.
>
> Only late in his life, shortly before the cessation of his labors in thinking, does the full scope required by such an inversion of Platonism become clear to him. That clarity waxes as Nietzsche grasps the necessity of the overturning, which is demanded by the task of overcoming nihilism. For that reason, when we elucidate the overturning of Platonism we must take the structure of Platonism as our point of departure. For Plato the supersensuous is the true world. It stands over all, as what sets the standard. The sensuous lies below, as the world of appearances. What stands over all is alone and from the start what

sets the standard; it is therefore what is desired. After the inversion – that is easy to calculate in a formal way – the sensuous, the world of appearances, stands above; the supersensuous, the true world, lies below. With a glance back to what we have already presented, however, we must keep a firm hold on the realization that the very talk of a 'true world' and 'world of appearances' no longer speaks the language of Plato.

But what does that mean – the sensuous stands above all? It means that it is the true, it is genuine being. If we take the inversion strictly in this sense, then the vacant niches of the 'above and below' are preserved, suffering only a change in occupancy, as it were. But as long as the 'above and below' define the formal structure of Platonism, Platonism in its essence perdures. The inversion does not achieve what it must, as an overcoming of nihilism, namely, an overcoming of Platonism in its very foundations. Such overcoming succeeds only when the 'above' in general is set aside as such, when the former positing of something true and desirable no longer arises, when the true world – in the sense of the ideal – is expunged. What happens when the true world is expunged? Does the apparent world still remain? No. For the apparent world can be what it is only as a counterpart of the true. If the true world collapses, so must the world of appearances. Only then is Platonism overcome, which is to say, inverted in such a way that philosophical thinking twists free of it. But then where does such thinking wind up?

During the time the overturning of Platonism became for Nietzsche a twisting free of it, madness befell him. Heretofore no one at all has recognized this reversal as Nietzsche's final step; neither has anyone perceived that the step is clearly taken only in his final creative year (1888).[7]

---

7 Martin Heidegger, *Nietzsche*, vols 1 and 2, trans. D. F. Krell (New York: Harper Collins, 1991), 200–2.

CHAPTER SEVEN

We should be aware that Platonism survives within the conceptions of 'hidden structure', the 'base' or 'infrastructure', the 'deep structure', and so on. Heidegger pointed out such a difficulty, but was he able to cut through the problem with his 'question of being' (*Seinsfrage*)? Where Nietzsche rejected the concept of 'Being', Heidegger recodes and reinterprets Nietzsche's thought ontologically. In other words, Heidegger unfortunately returns once more to what Nietzsche called this 'common philosophy of grammar'. This return shows us precisely the fundamental 'difficulty'.

In the end, Marx's inversion of Hegel's philosophy took place through the Hegelian vocabulary itself. However, is it not the case that, in *Capital*, it is precisely through this *loyalty* to Hegel that the most effective negation of the Hegelian system, compared to any other critique, became possible? To truly *read Capital* is to throw ourselves into the midst of this difficulty.

Index

absolute surplus value, 51, 52, 56
alienation, theory of, xvi, xx, 62, 65, 70, 73, 91
Althusser, Louis, 70
ancient capitalism, 31
Ancient Society (Morgan), xxxvii
'*Anpō* Struggle,' xxix–xxx
Architecture as Metaphor (Karatani), xvii
Aristotle, 29–30, 31, 33
Asada, Akira, xii, xvi

base, xxxvi–xxxvii, 68, 80, 86, 87, 88, 111. *See also* economic base
Bauer, Bruno, 70
Bonaparte, 80, 81, 84, 85, 86
Borromean knot of 'capital-nation-state,' xxv, xxvii

capital. *See also* capital-nation-state; industrial capital; merchant capital
  as able to overcome human will and persist, 55–6
  as ceaselessly creating margins, gaps, and differences, 58
  logic of, xx, xxi, xxiv, xxvi
  as only concerned with rate of profit, 50
  production of, xxiv
Capital: A Critique of Political Economy (Marx)
  according to Uno, xxx–xxxi
  brilliance of, 5
  as classic in history of political economy, 1
  as exemplifying Marx's economic thought, xx
  as intervention in philosophy, xvi

Karatani's reading of, xxxii, xxxix
  as Marx's reading of texts of classical political economy, 6
  non-Marxist economists' treatment of, 8
  nothing in text of as transparent, 66
  principal task of, 11
  as problematizing concept of text itself, 67
  role of, xxxii, xxxviii
  as theory of ideology, 76
capitalist production, 5, 50, 52, 59
capital-nation-state, xxv, xxvi, xxxvi, xxxviii
centre of possibility, according to Karatani, xviii
circulation
  described, 36
  parallax between circulation and production, xxiii–xxiv
  process of, 36, 42, 43, 44, 50, 56
  and production of capital, xxiv
  sphere of, xxvi, xxvii
class, concept of, 69–70, 86
class consciousness, 86
classical political economy
  Capital as Marx's reading of texts of, 6
  commodity in, 16, 18, 107
  on concept of surplus value, 56–7
  on concept of value, 88
  crisis as kind of rebuke to, 60
  as glorifying technical revolution, 58
  on how two qualitatively

different use-values could be equivalent, 32
industrial capitalism and, 63
labour theory of value as inherited from, xxxi
Marx as adopting theory of labour-time from, 36
Marx as differing from, 8, 11
Marx as inheriting and continuing project of numerous aspects of, 8
Marx's critique of, xxxv, 2, 31, 60, 61, 62
merchant capital according to, xxxiv
as nearly touching true relation of things without consciously formulating it, 90
as opposing theorists of mercantilism, 43
Proudhon as basing self on, 38
theory of equilibrium of, xxxv
treatment of money in, 37
as unable to achieve anything of note, 11
as unable to discover value-form, 59–60
class struggle, xxvii, 69, 79, 83, 88
class unconscious, 86
C–M', 38, 39, 50
C–M–C', 42
collective subjectivity, 46, 75
commodities
according to Marx, xxiii, xxxii, xxxiii, 4, 15–16
and chain of relative relationships, 21
in classical political economy, 16, 18, 107
as equal in value, 19–20
labour power as, 53
mysteriousness of, 76
relation of money to, 84–5
as text, 67
as value-form, 18–19
value of, 16, 17, 22, 30, 39, 44, 47, 53, 54–5, 91, 107, 109
commoditology (*shōhingaku*), 18

commodity economy, xiv, xxiii, 49, 54
commodity exchange, xxx, xxxiii, xxxvii, 43–4
commodity fetishism, 17
commodity-form, 15, 16, 63, 67
commodity production, 49, 54
communism, according to Marx, xxxvii–xxxviii, 100
consciousness, 17, 25, 26, 37, 38, 52, 74, 78, 86, 89, 92, 93, 94, 95, 96, 97, 100, 101. *See also* class consciousness; false consciousness; self-consciousness; teleological consciousness
crisis
according to Keynes, 62
defined, 63–4
Engel's theory of, 61
Marx's possibility of, 63
Marx's theory of, 61
in nineteenth century, 62–3
problematic of as lever for Marx's critique of classical political economy and Hegelian philosophy, 62, 63
use of term in Japanese language, 60n9
critical theory, x, xii, xv, xvii

Democritus, 6–8, 9, 67, 68
Derrida, Jacques, xvi, 95
Descartes, René, 104, 105
desire, 15–16, 86, 95
Deutsch–Französische Jahrbücher, 72
dialectic, 11, 22, 25–6, 33, 56, 84, 108–9
dialectical materialism, xvii, 1
différance, 95
The Difference Between the Democritean and Epicurean Philosophy of Nature (Marx), xxxii–xxxiii, 6, 10, 66, 68, 70
discourse of political economy, 88
division of labour, 57, 78, 98
Dostoevsky, Fyodor, 27

INDEX

economic base, xxx, xxxvi–xxxvii, xxxix, 68, 87
1844 Manuscripts (Marx), 60, 65, 70, 72, 91, 104
The Eighteenth Brumaire (Marx), 80–1, 82, 86, 88, 89
Engels, Friedrich, 5, 61, 70, 72, 99, 100
Epicurus, 6–8, 9, 10, 40, 67, 68, 95
equal exchange, xxxiv, 42–3, 44, 47, 52, 58
equivalent form, 20–1, 23, 28, 31
Essays (Montaigne), 2–4
essence, and phenomena, 90, 91.
exchange. *See also* commodity exchange; equal exchange; linguistic exchange; unequal exchange
  according to Marx, xxxi
  as based on mutual consent and contractual forms, 54
  direct exchange, 36, 38
  mediated exchange, 36
  modes of, xxvi, xxxvii–xxxviii, xxxix
  as not taking placing without equality, 29
  prioritizing of, xxiii, xxxi, xxxvii
  process of, 44, 45–6
exchange-value, 16, 18, 19, 26

false consciousness, 76
fetish (commodity), xxxi
Feuerbach, Ludwig, 70, 72, 87, 91, 92
Foucault, Michel, 63
French ideologues, 80
Freud, Sigmund, 25, 26, 60, 63, 64, 89, 93–4, 95, 97
Fukumoto Kazuo, xix

Gendai shisō: Revue de la pensée d'aujourd'hui, xii
German ideologues, 79
The German Ideology (Marx), 17, 68, 70, 71–2, 77, 79, 87, 98, 103–4
Gunzō (journal), xv

Hegel, G. W. F., xxxiii, 6, 8, 11–12, 28, 41, 60, 68, 71, 77, 81–2, 84, 90, 104, 108, 111
Heidegger, Martin, xli, 12, 109, 111
Heiner, Heinrich, 104
Hihyō kūkan (Critical Space), xii
Hiromatsu Wataru, xii, xvi, xviii, xxx, 70
historical materialism, xvii, xxx, xxxi, xxxvi, xxxvii, 1, 59, 70, 73
History of Philosophy (Hegel), 6
Hobbes, Thomas, 79
human equality, 30, 31–2, 33
human labour, 17, 20, 24, 25, 30, 31, 32, 97–8, 101
Husserl, Edmund, 75

identity
  direct identity, 36
  qualitative identity, 22, 46
  space of, 68
  turning qualitative difference into, 47, 59
ideology
  bourgeois ideology, 79
  described, 76–7
  historical materialism as, xxxi
  philosophy as meaning, 68, 71
  theory of, 76
  use of term, 88
'the *impasse* or *(im)possibility* of the commodification of labour power' (*rōdōryoku shōhinka no 'muri'*), xxii–xxiii
industrial capital, xxxiv, xxxviii, 43, 44, 49, 50, 55, 56, 57, 58, 63
infrastructure, 68, 69, 80, 87, 88, 111
interest rates, 50
interiority, xx, 36, 37
The Interpretation of Dreams (Freud), 26
Introduction to 'Capital' (*Shihonron nyūmon*) (Uno), xx
Introspection and Retrospection (Karatani), xvii
Investigations I (Karatani), xvii, xxxvi

Investigations II (Karatani), xvii, xxxvi

Jakobson, Roman, 42
Japan
  emergence of New Left movement in, xxix–xxx, xxxii
  postwar Japan as most Marxist country, xiii
  as second largest capitalist economy, xiv
Japan Communist Party, xxix
Japanese language, and concept of subject, 106n5

Keynes, John Maynard, 62
Kobayashi Hideo, 15
Kuhn, Thomas, 76–7

labour
  division of, 57, 78, 98
  human labour, 17, 20, 24, 25, 30, 31, 32, 97–8, 101
  necessary labour, 51, 52
  surplus labour, 51, 52
labour money, theory of, 38
labour power, ix, xxi, xxii, xxiii, xxiv, xxv–xxvi, xxviv, 30, 31, 44, 50–1, 53, 54, 55, 57, 58–9, 61, 62, 90, 98
labour time, 8, 35, 36, 51, 55
Lacan, Jacques, 25, 26
Langer, Susanne, 94–5
language
  as differential system, 95
  emergence of, 95
  Marx as problematizing status of, 87
Lassalle, Ferdinand, xxxii, 1–2, 13
Lenin, Vladimir, 98
Lévi-Strauss, Claude, 22, 89, 90, 92
linguistic exchange, xxxiii, xxxv–xxxvi, 42
linguistics, xvii, xxxiii, xxxv, xxxvi, xxxvii, 18, 22, 42, 46n7
Lukács, György, 86

M (money), 38
Malraux, André, xli

Mammon (capital), xxxi
Man, Paul de, xvi
'Marginal Revolution,' xxxv
Marukusu sono kanōsei no chūshin (Marx: Towards the Centre of Possibility) (Karatani), xi. See also *Marx sono kanōsei no chūshin* (Marx: Towards the Centre of Possibility) (Karatani) (1978)
Maruyama Masao, xvi
Marx, Karl
  critique of socialist idealism by, 32
  departure of from Germany, 73
  doctoral dissertation of, xxxii, 66, 68, 70–1. See also *The Difference Between the Democritean and Epicurean Philosophy of Nature* (Marx)
  dynamic intuition of, 89
  early Marx and late Marx, 65–6
  humanism of, 100
  as speaking of enigmatic nature of commodity, 15
Marx-Engels Collected Works (Kaizōsha edition), xix
Marx sono kanōsei no chūshin (Marx: Towards the Centre of Possibility) (Karatani), xv–xvii, xxiv. See also *Marukusu sono kanōsei no chūshin* (Marx: Towards the Centre of Possibility) (Karatani)
materialism
  dialectical materialism, xvii, 1
  historical materialism, xvii, xxx, xxxi, xxxvi, xxxvii, 1, 59, 70, 73
Mauss, Marcel, xxxvii
M–C, 38, 39, 50
M–C–M′, xxxiv, 42, 43, 47, 50
Menger, Carl, xxxv
merchant capital, xxxi, xxxiv, 38, 39–40, 43, 44, 47, 49, 50, 54, 55, 56, 58
Ministry of Trade and Information (MITI), xiv

INDEX

Minkowski, Hermann, 74
M–M′, 50
money
  according to Marx, 36
  conceptions of, 37–8
  dichotomy of 'phenomena and essence' as product of, 90
  emergence of according to Marx, 11
  metaphysics of, 24, 107
  relation of to commodity, 84–5
money-form, 19, 20, 21, 22, 23, 26, 29, 32, 33, 35, 36, 38, 39, 46–7, 51, 55, 59, 62, 63, 64, 90, 91, 107
Montaigne, Michel de, 2–4
Morgan, Lewis Henry, xxxvii

Natsume Soseki, 67
necessary labour, 51, 52
necessary labour time, 51
Neue Rheinische Zeitung, 75
New Left movement, in Japan, xxix–xxx, xxxii
Nietzsche, Friedrich, 9, 27, 28, 29, 77, 78, 95, 97, 105–6, 109, 110
number, concept of, 46–7

objective world, 74
objectivity, 75, 76
On the History of Religion and Philosophy in Germany (Heine), 104
opaque text, 39
Ōtsuka Hisao, xvi

Parsons, Talcott, 42
passional, 91–2
passionate being, 92, 94
Petty, William, 35
phenomena, essence and, 90, 91
philosopher, problematizing of, 77, 78
Philosophical Notebooks (Lenin), xx–xxi
philosophy
  de-centre of, 79
  discourse of, 76
  history of, 6, 8, 9, 61, 68, 69, 71

as inversion of value, 78
inverted interpretation of, 77–8
Philosophy of History (Hegel), 82
The Philosophy of Right (Hegel), 28
physical organization, 93, 95, 98
Plato, 37, 38, 45, 84, 90, 100, 108, 109–10, 111
political economy, discourse of, 88
preconscious, 97
Principles of Political Economy (Keizai genron) (Uno), xx
production
  capitalist production, 5, 50, 52, 59
  commodity production, 49, 54
  parallax between circulation and production, xxiii–xxiv
  process of, xxiv, xxvi, 43–4, 51, 56
profit, 38, 42, 49–50
Prolegomena to the Agrarian Question (Nōgyō mondai joron) (Uno), xx
proletariat, as commodity possessor, 54–5
Proudhon, Pierre-Joseph, 32, 38, 52

The Raw and the Cooked (Lévi-Strauss), 92
relation, concept of, 94, 95
relative surplus value, 51, 56, 59, 98, 99
relative value, 44, 59
representation, 94, 95, 98
representatives, 82, 83–4, 85
represented, 82, 83
Republic (Plato), 100
Ricardo, David, xxxv, 19, 31
Rousseau, Jean-Jacques, 27, 38
Ruge, Arnold, 72, 77

Sade, Marquis de, 27
Sakamoto Ryoma, 40
Sakisaka Itsurō, xix
Saussure, Ferdinand de, xxxiii–xxxiv, xxxv, 18, 21, 22, 24, 37, 42, 45, 95
script, 25, 26, 36, 37, 38, 42, 43, 88
self-consciousness, 4, 7, 95, 103

Shihonron no tetsugaku (The Philosophy of *Capital*) (Hiromatsu), xviii
signified, 18, 21, 23, 24, 107–9
signifier, 4, 9, 18, 21, 23, 24, 37, 78, 91, 94, 95, 107, 109
Smith, Adam, xxxiv, 8, 19, 31, 35, 60, 88
social relations, 74, 91
Stalinism, xxix, 65, 100
standpoints, according to Marx, 75–6
structuralism, xxxiii, 24, 89, 96
The Structure of World History (Karatani), xvii, xxxix
Studies on Hysteria (Freud), 26
suffering, 91–2, 93, 95, 100, 101, 102
superstructure, xxxi, xxxvi, 73, 86
surplus labour, 51, 52
surplus labour time, 51
surplus value, ix, xxxiv, 38, 41–2, 43, 44, 47, 49–51, 55, 56, 57, 58, 59, 63, 88. *See also* absolute surplus value; relative surplus value
Suzuki Kōichirō, xiii

Tanaka Kichiroku, 92–3
technical innovation, xxxiv, 57, 58
technical revolution, 58
teleological consciousness, 97, 98, 99, 101
telos, 97, 98
Theories of Surplus Value (Marx), 88
theory of alienation, xvi, xx, 62, 65, 70, 73, 91
theory of ideology, 76
theory of labour money, 38
theory of the value-form, xxxiii, 11, 12–13, 18, 25, 26, 35, 53, 61, 62, 85, 89, 90, 97, 109
Theory of Value (Uno), xx
Theses on Feuerbach (Marx), 70

Transcritique: On Kant and Marx (Karatani), xvii, xxxviii

unconscious, 25, 26, 58, 64. *See also* class unconscious
unequal exchange, xxxiv, 39, 42, 44
universal truths, 69, 79
University of Tokyo, economics department, xiii, xiv
Uno Kōzō, xii, xvi, xviii–xxii, xxx, xxxi, 61–2
use-value, 5, 16, 18, 19, 20, 21, 22, 23, 24, 26, 32, 57, 62, 98, 107, 109
US–Japan Joint Security Treaty (*Anpō*), xxix

Valéry, Paul, xxxii, 40–1, 67, 70, 104–5
value. *See also* surplus value; use-value
  Aristotle's understanding of according to Marx, 29–30
  classical political economy on concept of, 88
  of commodities, 16, 17, 22, 30, 39, 44, 47, 53, 54–5, 91, 107, 109
  expanded form of, 21
  labour theory of, 37
  philosophy as inversion of, 78
value-form, xxxiii, 10, 11, 12–13, 16, 17, 18, 19, 20, 21, 23, 24, 25, 26, 35, 37, 38, 45, 47, 53, 59, 61, 62, 63, 64, 85, 89, 90, 97, 109
Vico, Giambattista, 96

wage, 52, 53, 55, 58, 90
Walras, Léon, xxxv
working day, length of, 51, 56, 59

Yoshimoto Taka'aki, xxx
Young Hegelians, 7, 60, 70, 71, 74, 82, 104